ACPL ITEM
DISCARDED

P9-EDO-485

AUG 2 8 '67.

AUG 2 8 '67.

The Other Half of the Egg ～ ～ ～ ～ ～

by *Helen McCully, Jacques Pépin*
& William North Jayme

Drawings by
MEL KLAPHOLZ

The Other Half of the Egg~ ~ ~

Or *180 Ways to Use Up Extra Yolks or Whites*

M. BARROWS & COMPANY, INC.
Distributed by
William Morrow & Co., Inc.

NEW YORK   1967

Copyright © 1967 by M. Barrows & Company, Inc. All rights reserved. No part of this book may be reproduced or utilized in any form or by any means, electronic or mechanical, including photocopying, recording or by any information storage and retrieval system, without permission in writing from the Publisher. Inquiries should be addressed to M. Barrows & Company, Inc., 425 Park Avenue South, New York, N.Y. 10016. Published simultaneously in Canada by George J. McLeod Limited, Toronto. Printed in the United States of America. Library of Congress Catalog Card Number 67-19688

1411189

Dedicated to those splendid ladies who hatched us three chickens, with apologies for any brooding we may have caused them over the years

       ~ *Ethel Lowerison McCully*
       ~ *Jeanne Bourdeille Pépin*
       ~ *Catherine Ryley Jayme*

Contents

PART IV

Eggs and Their Other Halves in ∽ ∽ ∽

INTRODUCTION

IN THIS BEST of all possible worlds, there are two achievements that surely rank with the greatest of Pythagoras, Galileo, Darwin, Freud, Einstein, and Henri Soulé. They are feats of which few people seem to be aware.

The first is that of a black Australorp hen who, a couple of decades ago, entered the egg-laying contest at South Africa's Glen Agricultural College and, 365 days later, won—by producing a record 355 eggs. The other is that of a French gastronome named Grimod de la Reynière who once sat down and counted 685 known ways to serve what Australorps manufacture.

Brilliant as these accomplishments are, each suggests possible refinements. Hardly a cook is now in a kitchen who would not be grateful to a talented, if implausible, fowl that would lay only whites or only yolks, or, to a modern-day Reynière who would supply recipes for what to do when one has whites or yolks left over. And here, in fact, is THE OTHER HALF OF THE

9

EGG, or 180 ways to use up those extra yolks and whites. It took two to do the job—a Franco-American coalition. And it took a third, me, to talk them into it.

The problem is as old as Apicius. Practically everyone knows at least one or two ways to boil, poach, fry, scramble, or bake the composite egg—yolk and white together. But let the two become separated, and then what?

My personal knowledge of cooking is paltry and my knowledge of eggs is merely miscellaneous. Once at a cocktail party I heard from a nutritionist that yolks contain Vitamin A, which postpones senility. A calorie counter taught me that each yolk contains about 75 little pot-belly producers. In a crossword puzzle, I found out that the phrase "to egg on" has nothing to do with eggs but comes from a Norse verb, *eggian,* that means about what "to egg on" means. I know that if you have yolks left over, you can use them to paint in tempera, or that if you have leftover whites you can feed them to the cat, who is supposed to like them.

The only real egg *recipe* I ever found out on my own was explained to me by Sylvester Major, major-domo these many years to the household of Douglas Moore, the composer for whom I wrote the libretto of the opera, "Carry Nation." It uses leftover whites: Invite for dinner half as many guests as you have egg whites. Just before everyone sits down at the table, beat the whites till they are stiff. Stir in some orange marmalade, spoon the mixture into the buttered top of a double boiler, and abandon over a low flame. By the time everybody is ready for dessert—there it is, a sort of soufflé, to be served with or without custard topping. (Beware! Custards require yolks! The arithmetic of the separated egg is a relentless thing.) And, how much marmalade, you may ask? *Some* marmalade. To an instinctive cook like Sylvester, *some* is as functional a measurement as four tablespoons. One does not cook without *some* intuition.

I am, in short, an abysmally ignorant cook and ask, as a result, some of the most insidious questions. Such as, "Now what do I *do* with the other half of this egg?" (Having just added an extra yolk to commonplace scrambled eggs—rich, delicious, sophisticated.) In answer to the question, Helen McCully offered to show me the inner workings of a soufflé. But, "fold" in the whites, she said. Fold? Now really, how, and in fact, why, fold an egg white? Jacques Pépin, on another occasion, suggested that, if I ever intended to learn to make a sauce, I would have to learn the principle of a *liaison*. This I thought I already knew a little something about, but I had not previously considered it in terms of egg yolks.

It was in part my intemperate demands for answers to this kind of question that provoked this book. The authors allowed me to insert here and there my own way of expressing simple-minded things for the benefit of other simple-minded cooks. They went so far as to include an entire glossary of culinary terms for me and the likes of me. And they ended up by writing a whole cookbook, not just a book about how to cook an egg. And this is the *truth* about the other half of the egg: You need a real soup-to-dessert book to learn how to use it up. Helen McCully and Jacques Pépin know all about this. They are professionals who know cooking backwards and forwards, and they know eggs, you might say, inside out.

Jacques was born in France's gastronomic capital, Lyons, barely three decades ago, and arrived in America in 1960, following his rigorous education at the chopping boards and stoves of great kitchens. At the age of thirteen he was apprenticed to the head chef of the Grand Hôtel de l'Europe in Bourg-en-Bresse, in the homeland of Brillat-Savarin. In a short time he found himself at the Meurice in Paris, then at the Plaza Athenée, and finally at the Hôtel Matignon, Présidence du Conseil—no mere three-star restaurant but France's "White House" where Jacques was Chef de Cuisine to the then Premier Charles de Gaulle Himself (mark well *all* the upper-case letters).

Helen McCully had a grandfather who was a sea captain. He taught his family to live well no matter how little money the fleet sometimes brought in. Helen's childhood was spent in a town on the Bay of Fundy; the tales of it sound like Currier-and-Ives America. Homemade biscuits! Cakes! Puddings! Pies! Game! It was a family that dined as heartily as Brady at Delmonico's.

What lured the lady away from an obviously idyllic existence? A longing to show others how to live life with the same gastronomic gusto. For thirteen years Helen was Food Editor of *McCall's* Magazine. After giving instruction to some 18,000,000 readers each month on how to do everything from planning menus to washing dishes, she cried "Enough!" and withdrew to write books, this one among others, in a penthouse in Manhattan. Says Helen, who is five feet, two inches tall, "A penthouse makes me feel taller." She has since proceeded with unflagging culinary imagination to become the Food Editor of *House Beautiful* Magazine.

This, then, is not my book but Helen's and Jacques's. And now it is your book, too. Have fun with it. Save eggs with it. And in using it, as with all other endeavors, follow Mark Twain's famous advice: "Put all your eggs in the one basket—and watch that basket!"

WILLIAM NORTH JAYME

New York, 1967

PART I

The Two Halves of the Glossary ∿ ∿ ∿

Coming to Terms with the Egg

Glossary: Coming to Terms with Mysterious Words and Phrases

THE TWO HALVES OF THE GLOSSARY

Yes, we know, glossaries normally appear at the ends of books. But ours comes here in two sections of PART I—half a general discussion of eggs and half a proper alphabetical glossary of cooking terms. They come at the beginning for two reasons. First, our point of departure is eggs, and obviously a point of departure *is* the beginning. It is astonishing how much there is to know about an egg. Second, we assume other cooks not much more knowledgeable than I will be using this book. We think they will want to know what certain mysterious words and phrases mean before, rather than after, they collide with them in mid-recipe.

Cooking, to some of us, appears to have such a rarified vocabulary that it might as well be a foreign language. Much of it is French for which no one has ever bothered to devise an English translation! But explained by teachers such as Helen McCully and Jacques Pépin, no language could be easier to learn. It is merely a convenient code for ordinary practical information that would otherwise have to be repeated at length over and over again. Even the most experienced cooks can always do with a handy place to look up terms, techniques, and new tricks. The suggestion is that you not only refer to these glossaries but that you take a look *in advance* at what is in them to refer to. We have tried to provide everything you need to know, so that whenever you cook an egg—or half an egg—in any of our recipes, you will not inadvertently lay one.

W.N.J.

Coming to Terms
with the Egg

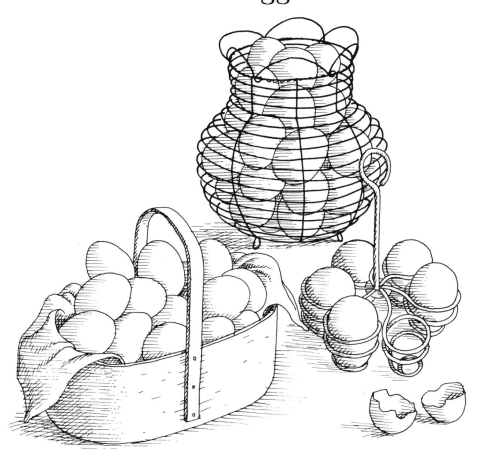

⌒ NOTE: *The entries in this glossary are listed in somewhat unorthodox fashion—that is, "chronologically," from the selection and buying of eggs through the storing, cooking, and serving of them.*

Grades. Eggs are graded according to quality and freshness. There are three grades: AA or Fancy Fresh, high-quality table eggs; Grade A, table eggs for baking and cooking; and Grade B. However, many fine eggs are sold under a brand name or trademark without a "letter" grade.

Grades AA and A are the most desirable for eating as eggs —cooked in the shell, poached, fried, or baked—because they will have the freshest flavor, and because the yolks will stay well rounded and well centered. Although Grade B is of a lower quality in these respects, such eggs have the same nutritive value and give the same cooking performance as Grades AA and A; they are, of course, more economical and can be used most satisfactorily in all egg cookery.

Sizes. Eggs of each grade are generally available in the following sizes: Extra-large, Large, Medium and Small. All sizes are available in all grades. One dozen extra-large eggs weigh 27 ounces; 12 large eggs, 24 ounces; 12 medium eggs, 21 ounces; and 12 small eggs, 18 ounces.

Small Versus Large. Weight for weight, small eggs are the equal of large eggs of the *same quality*. If a recipe calls for 1 large egg, you can usually substitute 2 small ones.

Shell Color. Color varies from white to deep brown because of pigment produced by the hen. Shell color does not affect the flavor, nutritive value, or cooking performance of the egg. Nor is it a dependable guide to yolk color. There is no advantage to paying more for brown or white eggs of the same quality and size.

Yolk Color. The color may vary from very pale yellow to very deep yellow or orange. Color has no effect whatsoever on the flavor or the nutritive value of eggs.

Calorie Count. One large egg (2 ounces) has 77 calories.

Volume Equivalents. From 4 to 6 shelled whole raw eggs, 8 to 10 raw egg whites, or 12 to 14 raw egg yolks will fill 1 standard measuring cup.

Storing Whole Eggs. To maintain freshness, eggs should always be stored in the refrigerator. Keep them in the carton or arrange them in the special egg container of the refrigerator, and do not place near them any strong-flavored food, since the shells are porous. Use eggs within 10 days to 2 weeks.

Storing Egg Whites. Egg whites freeze perfectly. Since 1 egg white fits neatly into an individual plastic ice-cube container, this is the ideal way to freeze them. It also makes it easy to tell at a glance how many whites you have on hand. Use a polyethylene bag to protect the frozen whites in the freezer. Thaw, and then use exactly as you would fresh egg whites. Allow about 30 minutes to thaw a single egg white frozen in a plastic container.

Storing Egg Yolks. Unlike egg whites, yolks will not freeze successfully. They can be stored uncooked for several days if placed intact in a container and covered with cold water. Or place each yolk in an individual plastic ice-cube container, with a seal of Saran right on top of the yolk so that no air can reach it. Refrigerate, of course. With either method, they should be used as soon as possible.

Cooked yolks can be stored for about a week. To cook, drop the unbroken yolks into simmering water; or put the yolks in a ramekin or custard cup, set it in simmering water, and cook until firm.

Room Temperature. Most authorities agree that egg whites should be brought to room temperature before using because they beat up faster and to a greater volume. This does not apply to egg yolks. The National Poultry and Egg Board suggests separating the eggs, placing the whites in a bowl, and then allowing them to come to room temperature. But if the yolks are not to be used immediately, follow directions for storing egg yolks in the preceding paragraph. If whole eggs to be cooked in the shell are not at room temperature, they can be cooked by the cold-water method (page 21). This forestalls the shells cracking, which happens when eggs straight from the refrigerator are started in boiling water.

Fat and the Egg White. Egg whites will not beat up stiffly if there is even the smallest particle of egg yolk in them, or if either the bowl in which they are beaten or the beater itself is moist or even slightly greasy. Fat, which egg yolk is, is the culprit.

Copper Bowls and the Egg White. French chefs and sophisticated cooks consider the unlined copper bowl and wire whisk the ideal utensils for beating egg whites. They say there is possibly some chemical reaction between whites and copper, because the results are very marked indeed. You get a greater bulk of "snow." Also there is less tendency to "graining" (when the beaten whites divide into fine particles and even liquify).

Removing Speck of Yolk From Whites. Take a piece of the egg shell and lift the speck or specks, as the case may be, from the whites. If this doesn't work, try to catch the yolk with a small piece of paper towel; usually the yolk will cling to the paper.

Time and Beaten Whites. Beaten whites won't stand for any length of time and, once they begin to thin out, it is impossible to bring them back to the required stiffness. Whites that have had sugar added before beating will remain firm much longer. A tight seal of Saran over the top of the bowl will also hold beaten whites for a while in case of emergency.

Folding Egg Whites into a Mixture. There are a good many circumstances in which you must know how to do this. The process is explained in detail in the soufflé section, on page 202.

Mixing Egg Yolks Into a Mixture. When you do this, you are making a *liaison*. See page 37.

Aluminum and Eggs. Yolks, whites, and whole eggs discolor when mixed, cooked, or molded in aluminum utensils because of the sulphur content of eggs. (Also, any dish that calls for wine tends to discolor when prepared in aluminum because of the acids present in the wine.) Heavy-bottomed enameled, stainless-steel, Pyrex, porcelain, or tin-lined copper pans are recommended.

Temperatures for Cooking. Eggs should always be cooked at low temperature, except omelets and *oeufs poêlés* or *frits* (French fried eggs) which are cooked at moderately high heat. Too much heat makes eggs tough and rubbery.

Boiled Eggs. The term "boil" in relation to eggs, whether soft or hard, has long since been abandoned because it implies high fast heat which, at best, can only lead to rubbery whites and discolored yolks, at the worst to cracked and leaking shells, water-logged and lopsided eggs.

Soft-Cooked Eggs. Perfectly cooked, the white is tender but solidified, and the hot yolk is liquid to semiliquid.

THE AMERICAN COLD-WATER METHOD: Place the egg, or eggs, straight from the refrigerator, in a saucepan deep enough to accommodate them without crowding. Add enough cold tap water to cover the eggs by at least a generous inch. Bring to a boil, 200° F. on a thermometer, uncovered, over high heat. This will take about 10 minutes or a little more. Take off the heat, cover, and let stand from 1 to 3 minutes. Timing depends on how firm you like the whites and yolks and can best be determined by trial and error. Plunge the cooked eggs into cold water to prevent any further cooking and to make them easier to shell.

THE AMERICAN BOILING-WATER METHOD: Bring 5 to 6 cups of water to a high boil; this may seem like a lot of water, but the eggs must be covered by at least an inch of water; also, if too little water is used, it will cool off too much when the eggs are added and the cooking time will not be long enough to cook the eggs to your taste. Lower the eggs into the water gently with a spoon, take the pan off the heat, cover, and allow to stand for 6 to 8 minutes. Cool as above. *Note*: If the eggs are cold, hold them under the hot-water tap briefly to take the refrigerator chill off them, otherwise they may crack.

THE FRENCH METHOD (*à la coque,* soft boiled): Plunge the eggs into boiling water and cook for 2½ to 3 minutes. Eggs should be at room temperature before cooking to forestall the shells cracking. Cool as indicated above.

Oeufs Mollets. Pronounced "moelay," literally translated, this means soft-boiled eggs, but "tender eggs" sounds more appealing. *Oeuf mollet,* one of the most delicious ways to eat an egg, is almost unknown in American homes. Eggs prepared in this way have been described as "betwixt and between" because they are simmered longer than soft-cooked eggs but not as long as hard-cooked ones. *Oeufs mollets* are frequently served cold in clear aspic (page 170), with salad greens and sauce vinaigrette (page 98), or hot on a bed of puréed spinach. They may also be served in any way that is suitable for poached eggs.

TO COOK OEUFS MOLLETS: Plunge eggs (they must be at room temperature) into a saucepan of boiling water deep enough so there is at least 1 inch of water above them. Cook, just below simmering, for 5½ to 6 minutes from the time the water comes to a boil again. Plunge immediately into cold water to keep the eggs from cooking further, and shell them when they are cool enough to handle. (See Shelling Cooked Eggs.)

TO KEEP SHELLED EGGS WARM: Place eggs gently in a pan of hot water, *not over heat.*

Hard-Cooked Eggs.

THE AMERICAN COLD-WATER METHOD: Follow instructions for soft-cooked eggs to the point where the water begins to show signs of reaching a rolling boil (200° F. on a thermometer). Reduce heat to simmer (180° to 200° F.) and hold this temperature for 12 minutes. Plunge eggs into cold water at once to stop the cooking. *Another way:* When water reaches a rolling boil, remove pan from heat, cover, and allow eggs to stand for 15 minutes. Cool immediately as above.

THE AMERICAN BOILING-WATER METHOD: Follow same instructions for soft-cooked eggs (boiling-water method), reducing heat to keep water simmering, and cook for 20 minutes. Cool immediately as above.

THE FRENCH METHOD (*dur,* hard): Plunge eggs into boiling water and cook for 8 to 10 minutes. Eggs should be at room temperature to prevent the shells cracking. Cool immediately as above.

TO KEEP PEELED EGGS WARM: Hard-cook eggs by any method, then place the peeled eggs in a pan of hot water, not over direct heat.

The French have many imaginative ways of serving hard-cooked eggs hot. Here are a few:

OEUFS AURORE. To 1 cup Sauce Velouté (see Glossary) add 4 tablespoons tomato paste. Coat the hard-cooked eggs with this sauce, sprinkle with grated cheese, and slide under the broiler until lightly glazed.

OEUFS BOULANGÈRE. Cut a small hard roll into halves and scoop out the soft insides. Fill with hard-cooked eggs, diced and mixed with Sauce Béchamel (see Glossary). Sprinkle with cheese, chopped cooked egg yolk, and chopped parsley.

OEUFS BRETONNE. Combine chopped sautéed mushrooms and finely chopped onions and leeks cooked together in butter. Cover the bottom of a baking dish with part of this mixture. Place halved hard-cooked eggs on top, and cover with remaining sauce. Place in a 400° F. oven long enough to heat through.

OEUFS À LA CHIMAY (page 175).

Shelling Cooked Eggs. The reason eggs are sometimes hard to shell is that they are very fresh. Two days in the refrigerator changes the acid-alkaline balance so the shell is less reluctant to leave the cooked egg. To shell, either soft- or hard-cooked eggs, hot or cold, crackle the shell gently on a flat surface or with the back of a spoon, taking care not to break the egg itself. Holding an egg in the palm of one hand, pull the shell and membrane from the egg, dipping it into water if necessary to help ease the shell off. Shelled hard-cooked eggs can be refrigerated for 2 days, but no longer. Soft-cooked eggs can be stored in the refrigerator in cold water, which helps to keep their shape, for the same length of time. They can be reheated as you would reheat poached eggs (page 28).

Fried Eggs. In France fried eggs can mean two things: *poêlés,* which are similar to American fried eggs, and *frits,* which are fried in deep fat or oil. In the United States we, too, fry eggs by two somewhat different methods. When frying eggs, it is well to remember that they start to cook from the bottom, before the top sets, so be careful not to let them get overcooked on the bottom.

TO FRY EGGS, AMERICAN STYLE: Heat butter, salad oil (or a combination of both, half and half), or bacon fat in a small frying pan; use 1 to 2 tablespoons for each egg. When the fat is sending off a pale-blue smoke, slip the eggs, one at a time, from a saucer into the fat; cook only 2 eggs at a time. Reduce heat to low. Baste the eggs with the hot fat until the whites are firm and the yolks show a light film over the surface. At this point, the yolks will still be liquid when pierced with a fork. Serve "sunny-side up," or turn at this point and cook for a few seconds longer. Season with salt and pepper.

ANOTHER AMERICAN METHOD: Heat the fat and pan until moderately hot. Break the egg directly into the pan, holding the shell as close to the surface of the pan as possible and letting the egg slip out gently. Cook over moderate heat and baste with the hot fat or turn the egg over; or add ½ teaspoon water for each egg, cover the pan, and steam the eggs. Cook to the degree of firmess you want. With this method the eggs will not be browned on the bottom.

OEUFS POÊLÉS. Melt a lump of butter in a hot skillet. When foaming, add eggs, previously broken into a saucer or plate, and cook very fast, shaking the pan constantly to avoid sticking. Slide onto a warm plate and serve "sunny-side up," seasoned with salt and freshly ground white pepper. Or, add a teaspoon of vinegar to the browned butter and pour over the eggs; this is called *oeufs au beurre noir*.

OEUFS FRITS: Use a small deep pan, small because you should only deep fry 1 egg at a time. Heat oil or lard, enough for the egg to "swim," to the smoking point. Break the egg—freshness is of the essence—into a saucer or plate and slide the egg into the hot fat to cook in this fashion. Roll the egg over with 2 wooden spoons or spatulas to gather the white around the yolk and to keep the natural shape of the egg. Fry for 2 to 2½ minutes. Drain well on a fresh towel. Season with salt and freshly ground white pepper; serve with crisp bacon or fried tomatoes. *Oeufs frits* puff up like fritters and are perfectly delicious served on a bed of puréed spinach or potatoes with sausages, or accompanied by fried bread and tomato sauce.

Broiled Eggs. Grease a shallow skillet or flameproof baking dish with a film of butter. When sizzling hot, break eggs into a sauce dish (Jacques means a saucer) and slip them into the skillet. Cook over direct heat for a minute, or until the edges just begin to turn white. Place in a preheated broiler and broil at medium temperature for 2 to 4 minutes, or until eggs are done to your taste.

WITH CREAM: Spoon 1 tablespoon heavy cream over each egg before placing eggs under the broiler.

WITH CHEESE OR CRUMBS: Sprinkle 1 teaspoon grated cheese or fine buttered bread crumbs over each egg before placing in the broiler.

Scrambled Eggs. Oeufs brouillés in French. Almost everyone has his own method for scrambling eggs and each thinks his is the right and proper one. Whatever the method, allow 2 eggs per person.

STANDARD UNITED STATES METHOD: For each egg, allow 1 tablespoon of milk, cream, water, or juice, and a pinch each of salt and pepper. Mix together with a fork—thoroughly if you want a uniform yellow, or slightly if you want the eggs streaked with white and yellow. Heat 1 tablespoon butter or oil in a small skillet until just hot enough to sizzle a drop of water. Add the egg mixture, reduce heat to moderate, and cook, lifting the mixture from the bottom and sides to allow the uncooked liquid to flow onto the pan. Cook until eggs are thickened to the degree you like them but still moist, from 5 to 8 minutes.

HELEN'S METHOD: Melt a good lump of butter in a heavy saucepan, add the well-mixed seasoned eggs (no liquid), and stir with a wooden spatula over very low heat until the eggs just start to thicken. Stir in another lump of butter, take off the heat, and continue to stir (the heat from the saucepan continues to cook the eggs) until you have a smooth creamy mixture. If the eggs must stand for any length of time, stir in 1 whole raw egg just before spooning the mixture onto a warm platter. This little trick helps to keep scrambled eggs moist and soft. You can vary scrambled eggs with minced fresh herbs (chives, tarragon, parsley, chervil, etc.) or thinly sliced truffles; stir into the eggs just before putting them in the skillet.

JACQUES'S METHOD: Beat eggs with a wire whip in the top of a double boiler; add salt and freshly ground pepper to taste. Place over simmering water and cook, stirring constantly, until cooked but still soft. Add 1 tablespoon heavy cream and a little nut of butter. Serve immediately.

Variations for OEUFS BROUILLÉS:

AUX CHAMPIGNONS: Garnish with sautéed diced mushrooms.

À L'ESPAGNOLE: Garnish with diced fresh tomatoes and a julienne of sweet peppers, both cooked in salad oil, on top.

AUX FINES HERBES: Stir minced fresh herbs into the eggs as in Helen's method (see above).

GRAND'MÈRE: Garnish with diced fried bread (croutons; see Glossary) and chopped parsley.

MAGDA: Stir chopped parsley and grated cheese into the eggs before cooking and garnish with croutons (see Glossary).

PARMESAN: Mix freshly grated Parmesan cheese into the eggs before cooking.

PORTUGAISE: Arrange a bouquet of *Tomates Concassées* (see Glossary) on the eggs after they are cooked.

Shirred Eggs. *Sur le plat,* eggs on the plate in French. Eggs cooked in this way are a "kind of poached egg whose merit depends on just the right degree of cooking." Right degree hinges on three points: (1) cooking the white until it becomes milky; (2) the shining mirrorlike quality of the yolk—in France *oeufs sur le plat* are sometimes called *oeufs au miroir* (looking-glass eggs)—which is achieved by putting the eggs in the oven for a few seconds or until the yolks look varnished;

(3) taking care to keep the eggs from sticking to the bottom of the plate.

Butter a small round or oval baking dish. Season the dish with salt and freshly ground pepper; never season the top of the eggs because it marks them with little spots. When butter is hot, break 2 eggs into the dish and cook slowly on top of the stove. For *oeufs au miroir,* place the dish in a hot oven for 45 to 50 seconds after eggs are cooked to glaze the top of the yolks.

Of the innumerable ways to garnish OEUFS SUR LE PLAT, *we give you a handful:*

À L'AMÉRICAINE: (1) Place a slice of grilled ham in the dish, and break the egg over it. When cooked, surround with a "thread" of tomato sauce (see Glossary). (2) Arrange pieces of cooked lobster on the bottom of the dish; break the egg over the lobster, and cook; to serve, surround with Sauce Américaine (page 208).

AUX ANCHOIS: Arrange diced anchovy fillets on the bottom of the dish; add the egg. When cooked, surround with more anchovy fillets.

WITH BACON: Arrange cooked bacon on the bottom of the dish, break the egg on top, and finish.

BERCY: When the egg is cooked, garnish with small grilled sausages and a "thread" of tomato sauce (see Glossary).

FLORENTINE: Break the egg onto a layer of blanched spinach leaves tossed in butter. Sprinkle all with grated cheese and coat the egg with Sauce Mornay (page 84). Bake in a 400° F. oven for 10 minutes.

Poached Eggs. Oeufs pochés in French.

THE AMERICAN METHOD: Fill a frying pan or shallow skillet three-fourths full of water. Add or omit, as you like, 1 tablespoon vinegar to 1 quart water. Bring to a boil, then reduce heat to simmer, the temperature at which the eggs should cook throughout. Break each egg separately into a cup or saucer and slip the egg from it into the water, holding the dish as close to the surface of the water as comfortably possible.

Poach for 3 to 5 minutes, depending on the firmness wanted, or until the white solidifies sufficiently to enclose the yolk and permits handling of the egg. Lift out of the water with a slotted pancake turner or slotted spoon and drain on paper towels.

TO TRIM A POACHED EGG: Cover your left hand with a clean dry cloth, lift the egg with the slotted spoon into the palm of this hand, and trim with a sharp knife or a pair of scissors. If not used immediately, keep the egg warm in hot water. Otherwise, slip the trimmed egg onto the dish or the toast, according to how it is going to be served.

THE FRENCH METHOD: Use a wide shallow pan (8 inches wide, 3 inches deep). Pour 3 to 4 cups water and ½ cup white vinegar (vinegar helps to "firm" the whites) into the pan and bring to a boil. Break eggs, one at a time, into a saucer or plate and slip each egg into the boiling water. Cook no more than 4 eggs at one time. Turn the heat down, allowing the water barely to simmer, or "shiver" (*frémir*). As eggs cook, drag the bottom of a large metal spoon or skimmer across the surface of the water to move the eggs and to keep them from sticking to the bottom of the pan. Cook for 2½ to 3 minutes. At this point, the whites should be set and the yolks soft to the touch. Lift from the hot water with a slotted spoon and place in a bowl of ice water. This washes off the vinegar and stops the cooking. When cool enough to handle, trim (see above). Place back in the ice water. Once cold, *oeufs pochés* can be kept in cold water, refrigerated, for several days. To serve cold, always drain on a clean towel before using. To serve hot, place egg or eggs in a strainer and heat in a pan of boiling water for about 1 minute. Drain before using.

Eggs in Ramekins. Oeufs en cocotte in French. Butter small porcelain ramekins (*ramequins* in French) or soufflé molds, then sprinkle with salt and freshly ground white pepper. Break an egg into each. Set the ramekins in a shallow pan with enough hot water to reach to two thirds of the depth of the ramekins. Cover tightly, bring water to a boil, and cook for about 3 minutes.

BAKED EGGS IN RAMEKINS: Place the ramekins in a preheated 350° F. oven and bake for 4 to 5 minutes. Take care when you remove the cover to see that no water drops into the cocottes.

OEUFS EN COCOTTE *are garnished in many ways. A few examples:*

À LA CRÈME: When cooked, the eggs are finished with a "thread" of thick cream.

DIPLOMATE: The bottom of the cocotte is garnished with a slice of *foie gras,* and a "thread" of tomato sauce (see Glossary) is added when the egg is done.

PORTUGAISE: Diced tomatoes tossed in butter with chopped shallots are placed in the bottom of the ramekin with a "thread" of tomato sauce (see Glossary).

Molded Eggs. Oeufs moulés in French. Coat molds large enough to hold an egg with soft, but not melted, butter, and sprinkle lightly with salt and freshly ground white pepper. Break the eggs into the molds. Set the molds in a pan of water, as for eggs in ramekins (above), and cook for 5 to 6 minutes. Allow to stand briefly before unmolding. Serve as you would *oeufs pochés* or *oeufs mollets.* Any small mold that gives a shape is suitable.

Omelets. Omelet making is both very simple and very difficult. Omelets can be well done, "just done," or *baveuses,* which means still running. It's all a matter of taste. Most experts, and all chefs, recommend using a pan that is used exclusively to make omelets. The point of this is that the surface of the pan is always smooth, there is no danger of the omelet sticking, and it will slide out of the pan with "the greatest of ease."

Break eggs into a bowl, season with salt and freshly ground white pepper, and beat with a fork until the mixture is very homogeneous. Place a lump of butter in the omelet pan; when just beginning to darken, or *noisette,* add the eggs. Holding the pan in the left hand, agitate it back and forth, at an angle, in a continuous movement; at the same time, stir the eggs briskly with the flat side of a fork held in the right hand. When cooked, but still soft on top, start to turn the "lip" on one side and roll down the omelet. Then tap the handle of the pan to encourage the omelet to fold onto itself, taking care that it comes to a point at each end. Turn it upside down onto a warm, not hot, platter, and garnish. The same garnishes used for all other French egg dishes can be used for omelets.

Serving Eggs.   All egg dishes should be served on warm, not hot, plates. On a hot dish, the eggs would go right on cooking.

Glossary: Coming to Terms with Mysterious Words and Phrases

NOTE: *The entries in this glossary are listed alphabetically.*

Apricot Glaze. In a saucepan, combine one 12-ounce jar of apricot jam with ½ cup sugar and ½ cup water. Cook over moderate heat, stirring constantly, for 5 minutes. Strain through a fine sieve, and stir in Cognac, Grand Mariner, or kirsch to taste. Cool. Apricot glaze is used extensively in pastry making by European chefs. This apricot glaze is also delicious as a sauce served warm over ice cream or steamed puddings.

Aspic. There are many explanations for the origin of the word. The most plausible is that it derives from the Greek, *aspis,* which means shield. Originally, aspic referred only to a decorated dish coated with or molded in jelly. Today, it is used interchangeably for the dish or the jelly itself (*gelée* in French), and either aspic or jelly is used to refer to the mixture, whether it is in liquid or jellied form. Our recipe for aspic is given on page 170.

GLAZING OR LINING MOLDS WITH ASPIC: This calls for a firmer *gelée* than that used merely for decoration. The proportions are 1 envelope of unflavored gelatin for each 1½ cups of liquid. Place a very small amount of the still liquid (or melted) aspic in a bowl, and stir over cracked ice or ice cubes until you "feel" the jelly starting to coat the spoon and the bottom of the bowl. At this point, the jelly becomes very syrupy. This happens very fast, which is why it is best to work with only a small amount at a time and to work quickly. Holding the mold on ice, spoon some jelly into it, then turn the mold so the jelly runs around the sides and covers the bottom. When almost firm, repeat, and repeat two or three more times, until the mold is completely lined with a "shell" of jelly. Chill until it is almost set and feels "sticky" to the finger.

Arrange any decorations on the bottom and sides, dipping them first into more (liquid) jelly so they will adhere. Chill again to the "sticky" stage. Fill the mold with whatever mixture you have made for your aspic; it should be as cold as (or colder than) the lined mold.

If the jelly hardens while you work, it can be softened over hot water or melted down, then brought back to the right consistency again over ice.

UNMOLDING COLD DISHES IN ASPIC: Cold food is inclined to cling tenaciously to the mold. One method is to dip the bottom of the mold into hot water for a few seconds to loosen it. Wipe the mold, then place the serving platter, upside down, over it. Then, holding platter and mold tightly together, turn them right side up. Or, you can invert the mold onto the platter and then wrap the bottom of the mold with hot damp cloths; be careful not to apply the heat for too long, or you may destroy the mold's design. Metal unmolds more easily than earthenware because metal conducts heat more quickly. Sometimes molds are available that have a tiny hole in the bottom. Blow through the hole, and *voilà!*

Unmolding hot dishes is somewhat easier; see page 43.

Béchamel, Sauce Béchamel.   (See also Velouté in this Glossary). Sauce Béchamel is to the French cook what white sauce is to the American—a major sauce that is the basis of an incredible number of recipes, both sweet and savory.

The thickening agent is the *roux*—flour and fat that are cooked together slowly before any liquid is added. Chefs cook the *roux* in a 350° F. oven for 10 to 15 minutes, before adding the liquid, if the final sauce is to be kept for any length of time. This method is probably of less interest to the home cook than it is to the professional who must always keep a supply of Béchamel on hand.

The point, though, and worth knowing, is that a Béchamel may thin out and become watery if the *roux* is not thoroughly cooked. Our recipe calls for cooking it in a saucepan on the top of the stove. If the Béchamel is to be used immediately— in a soufflé, for example—the *roux* need be cooked only about 3 minutes, but it must be cooked, otherwise the finished product will taste raw and "floury." A *roux* may be cooked up to 6 or 8 minutes (see *roux blanc* under Liaison in this Glossary).

The thickness of a Béchamel is in direct relation to the proportion of flour per cup of liquid.

	FLOUR	LIQUID
thin sauce	1 tablespoon	1 cup
medium sauce	1½ tablespoons	1 cup

	FLOUR	LIQUID
thick sauce	2 tablespoons	1 cup
heavy sauce	3 tablespoons	1 cup

The amount of fat varies according to the recipe in which the Béchamel is to be used; we have specified the proportions wherever the sauce is used in our recipes.

To make a Béchamel: Melt fat in a heavy saucepan (not aluminum) over low heat. Blend in the flour and cook slowly, stirring constantly, until the fat and flour froth—about 3 minutes—without browning (this is the white *roux,* or *roux blanc*). Take off the heat, add the liquid, and beat vigorously with a wire whip to incorporate the *roux* thoroughly. Put back over moderately high heat and cook, stirring with a whip, until the Béchamel comes to a boil. Boil for 1 minute, stirring constantly. Take off the heat and whip in the seasonings.

If a Béchamel must stand briefly before it is used, cover the surface of the sauce with a piece of Saran to prevent a skin forming on top. Or, butter it as chefs do: stick a fork into a lump of hard butter and rub it lightly over the surface of the sauce.

Blanch. The opposite of refresh, *q.v.* The purpose of blanching is to soften or wilt foods; to reduce strong flavors, such as garlic, onion, bacon, cabbage; or to loosen the skins of peaches, tomatoes, nuts. Generally, food is blanched by plunging it briefly into boiling water.

Broth, Bouillon, and Stock—are They the Same Thing? In the kitchen, yes, or at least cooks use the terms interchangeably and one basic definition applies to them all. They are the liquid obtained from simmering meats, bones, poultry, or fish trimmings with vegetables, seasonings, and water. This liquid, strained and often reduced, is the base for soups, sauces, consommés, and aspics, and it is also used to braise meats and to cook vegetables. Bouillon is the French word, now anglicized, for stock or broth.

The basic definition, however, covers an inordinate number of different kinds of flavorful liquids. The broth obtained from poaching fish fillets for 20 minutes or from boiling pounds of beef and bones for many hours, and every variation in between, are all included. For this reason, it is a temptation to specify a category for each of the three terms. But this cannot be done in ordinary English usage today.

What can be done is to specify what each of the three terms *cannot* apply to. Broth and bouillon (the latter both in this country and in France) are also used to describe a clear liquid that is ready to serve as a soup. But broth may also mean a thick soup, or almost any soup. It is the most general term of the three. Bouillon may not be so loosely used; it must be clear, or more or less so.

A stock may in actual fact be a soup (a more or less clear one), but it may not be referred to as stock once it is served. Magically, whenever we bring a good chicken stock to the table, we change its name to soup, broth, or bouillon. Stock, in other words, is the one strictly kitchen term of the three.

The recipes in this book use the three kitchen terms interchangeably, for homemade or canned products or for cooking liquids produced in the course of the recipe.

Butter. **1411189**

SWEET *versus* SALTED: Jacques, like most Frenchmen, doesn't particularly care for salted butter. Salt is added as a preservative, and salted butter, accordingly, may not always be fresh. Sweet butter, on the other hand, always gives its age away by turning rancid. Sweet butter is made from matured cream, is left unsalted, and has a kind of nutty flavor.

CLARIFIED BUTTER: This is ordinary butter that has been heated until it melts and the milky residue sinks to the bottom of the pan. The clear yellow liquid that sits on top is clarified butter.

To clarify, cut the butter into pieces and place in a saucepan over moderate heat. When it has melted and foamed, allow it to rest so the clear liquid will rise to the top. Then pour this off slowly and carefully so the milky residue is left in the bottom of the pan.

Chocolate Glaze. Melt (see below) 2 squares (1-ounce size) each of unsweetened and semisweet chocolate over hot, *not boiling,* water. Stir in 2 teaspoons honey and 4 tablespoons softened butter and stir until the butter melts.

Chocolate, to Melt. Like most professionals, Jacques melts chocolate over low direct heat, but the nonprofessional is advised to melt it over hot water—not boiling water, which may cause steam to rise and condense. Chocolate is a fat and, as everybody knows, fat and water won't mix. If even a few drops of water get into the melting chocolate, it will tighten and become impossible to use. The mess can be salvaged, however, by adding one or two tablespoons of vegetable shortening (not butter, which only adds additional moisture), then stirring until the chocolate has reliquified.

Cool versus Chill. Cool simply means to set aside a hot dish and allow it to stand at room temperature until it is no longer warm to the touch. Chill, on the other hand, means to refrigerate until cold.

Court Bouillon. A seasoned broth in which to cook fish, shellfish and, in some instances, vegetables. There is one recipe for *court bouillon* in this book (for cooking lobster) on page 176.

Crème Chantilly. This is heavy cream, whipped, sweetened to taste with confectioners' sugar, and perfumed with vanilla, rum, or a liqueur. If available, it is best to use cream that is two days old because it will whip into a heavier mixture. This is important if the crème is to be piped onto a dish with a pastry tube.

Crème, Sauce Crème. This is sauce Béchamel enriched with cream. To make about 2 cups sauce crème, make sauce Béchamel (page 33) in these proportions: 3 tablespoons flour, 2½ tablespoons butter, 1½ cups milk, seasoned with salt and freshly ground white pepper. When the sauce is completed, beat into it ½ cup heavy cream and a few drops of lemon juice. Can be served with vegetables, fish, eggs, poultry.

Croutons. Cut white bread into ½-inch cubes. Fry in butter and peanut or other salad oil, half and half, until golden all over.

Drain on paper towels. Croutons are used to garnish many dishes, including soups, eggs, entrées.

Double boiler. Jacques's and France's word for it is *bain-marie.* The French chef's *bain-marie* is not really quite the same, being a large open pan filled with hot water into which one or several saucepans are set. The double boiler that we know can be used in two ways—ours, and by the French method.

In the United States, we always say "cook *over* boiling water," putting only about 2 inches of water in the bottom pan and not allowing the top pan to touch the water. But *Larousse Gastronomique* says of the *bain-marie* method that it "consists of cooking in a receptacle, in a casserole or pan, *filled* with water kept near the boiling point." To cook this way in the home double boiler simply means filling the bottom pan so that the top pan rests *in* the hot water.

Jacques follows the French method—fine for a chef but chancy for the home cook, who rarely works with the speed and assurance of the professional. Cooking with the pan above the boiling water is, of course, slower.

Foods are also kept warm in a *bain-marie,* or in a double boiler *over* hot water.

Garlic. Whether you peel it or not depends on the recipe. If you are using garlic in a sauce that will be strained, peeling is not always necessary. This is true of onions, too. In any recipe calling for chopped garlic, peeling is essential. When the recipe calls for crushed garlic, the professional chef often simply mashes it, unpeeled, with a cleaver. The garlic press is a good household device for mashing, but it is well to remember that garlic from a press is three times as strong as garlic that has been minced or chopped.

To remove garlic odor from hands, rub fingers with lemon juice.

Liaison. The professional term for the thickening agent that binds ingredients together to bring sauces and soups to the right consistency. The four *liaison* agents used in this book are *beurre manié, roux (blanc* and *brun),* arrowroot, and egg yolks.

BEURRE MANIÉ is a raw or uncooked *roux*—a mixture of fresh butter and flour kneaded together, in some cases with more flour than fat. When you have a sauce that does not have the right consistency, you add a little *beurre manié*—a *noisette,* or "little nut"—to bring it to the perfect stage. You add it at the last moment; or use it when you make a fast sauce that is to be served right away. Do not use it in a sauce that is to be kept or reheated—a Béchamel or white sauce, for example—because the sauce might thin out and become watery. After a *beurre manié* has been added, the sauce must be cooked for an additional 8 to 10 minutes or it will taste raw and floury.

ROUX, also a mixture of fat and flour, is cooked before it is combined with the liquid, so that the finished sauce can be reheated and still keep its consistency. A *roux blanc* should be cooked slowly for 6 to 8 minutes without allowing it to brown. A *roux brun* is also cooked slowly, but longer, until it turns a rich nut brown.

ARROWROOT must be mixed with a cold liquid—water, stock, or wine, depending on the dish you are making—until smooth. Then stir the mixture into the sauce, and cook only until the sauce is clear and transparent, a matter of minutes. This lovely translucent quality is the main advantage in using arrowroot. Allow about 1 tablespoon to ¾ to 1 cup of liquid. (This is less than the amount of flour you would use for the same amount of liquid.) Sauces thickened with arrowroot reach their maximum thickness at 175° F. to 190° F. on the thermometer.

EGG YOLKS: When yolks are used to thicken sauces and soups, they are usually whipped into cold milk or cream, or some other cold liquid, before being incorporated into the hot mixture. Jacques emphasizes that cooking with egg yolks is tricky, and that they will curdle and turn granular unless beaten first with a cold liquid, very gradually combined with the hot mixture, then heated slowly. The experienced chef will put the *liaison* directly into the sauce or soup, but the amateur may find a less direct process safer. To make the *liaison*, first mix the yolks and liquid in a bowl with a wire whip. Then add about 2 ladles or cups of the hot sauce in a thin steady stream, mixing quickly and steadily all the while. Finally, pour this mixture back into the sauce, whipping constantly to prevent patches and fragments of egg yolk in the finished sauce. If patches do occur, simply strain the sauce or soup through a fine sieve or several layers of cheesecloth.

Makes Ribbons. This is the term used to describe the mixture when egg yolks and sugar are beaten together to the perfect consistency. All that's meant is that the mixture should be beaten to the point where it is pale yellow and thick enough to fall back on itself, which makes "ribbons" that dissolve slowly.

Marchand de Vins Sauce. Heat 2 tablespoons butter in a small saucepan. Add 3 tablespoons minced shallots, and cook until tender but not brown. Add ¾ cup dry red wine, and reduce the sauce, over high heat, to half its original quantity. Stir in ¾ cup canned brown gravy, bring to a boil, and simmer for a couple of minutes. Taste for seasoning. Before serving, stir in a tablespoon of butter.

Mussels. Mussels call for muscle. They must be cleaned with the greatest possible care to remove all sand from their interiors and to rid the shells of any slime or dirt which might spoil the juices. And mussels (those you've gathered yourself or those from the fishmonger) that are not shut tight, or those that feel lighter than their compatriots, should be discarded; also those that seem especially heavy, because the chances are they are enclosing sand rather than that lovely flesh. Each mussel should be scrubbed with a rough brush under running water and any encrustations scraped off with a small sharp knife, leaving the shell absolutely clean. The beard, which resembles old dried grass, must be cut off. After the first cleaning, drop the mussels into a pail of fresh water for a couple of hours so they will throw off any sand they have and lose a bit of their saltiness. Always, when you drain mussels, lift them from the water. Do not drain through a colander or you will collect the sand in the bottom of the pail. After this interlude, mussels should be washed and drained a second time before cooking.

Mussels are sold by weight; figure on 10 to 12 per pound.

Onions. Recipes often call for chopped onions to be cooked in butter until they are "limp and transparent," without browning. Chefs have a nice trick for this: Melt the butter in the pan, add the onion, then add ½ cup or so of water. Place over moderate heat and cook until all the water has evaporated. If the onions are not limp and transparent at this point, add more water and continue cooking until water has evaporated.

Pepper. The French use freshly ground white pepper n ore than black—according to Jacques "for aesthetic reasons." In a white dish where color is important, white is always used. Otherwise, either black or white.

Petits Fours Secs. These are small crisp cakes that are baked in a slow oven. Essentially biscuits, or what we call cookies, but usually more delicate and more elegant.

Purée. Essentially, puréeing is the same as mashing. You can purée foods through a food mill, through a sieve, in a mortar, or with a potato masher. Sometimes the purée can be made in an electric blender, depending on what is being puréed. Heavy, compact foods are apt to put too much of a strain on the motor unless sufficient liquid is added. Others, however, may be too fragile and will be liquified rather than puréed by the blender; they will keep a better texture if puréed some other way.

Reducing. Not you—liquids. The term simply means to boil down a liquid to reduce the quantity and to concentrate the flavors. A well-written recipe indicates the extent to which the liquid should be reduced—especially important if one is making sauces.

Refresh. From the French *rafraîchir,* and the opposite of blanch, *q.v.* Lettuce is refreshed when it's washed. Hot foods that must be cooled quickly in cold water to stop the cooking are refreshed.

Sauces. Any book concerning eggs must have a lot to say about sauces. Without eggs, especially egg yolks, much of sauce cookery would not exist. See Liaison in this Glossary; the section on yolks in sauces starting on page 83; and see in this Glossary the Béchamel, Crème, Marchand de Vins, Tomato, and Velouté sauces which, though they do not all contain eggs, are basic and used repeatedly, most especially the Béchamel. Eggs—whole, yolks, whites—are used in still more sauces listed in the Index.

Sauté. To sautè something is often confused with frying it but the two processes couldn't be more different. Fry means to cook foods in a considerable amount of fat and also to fry in deep fat. Sauté means to cook in a very small amount of very hot fat. Food can be sautéed just to brown it, or to cook it all the way through. Whatever fat is used—butter, oil, or butter and oil—it must be almost smoking to seal in the juices. Otherwise, the juices escape and the food won't brown. Also, the food must be dry. If it's too damp, steam develops which impedes browning. It's important, too, not to crowd the pan when sautéing meat. There should be air between the pieces or they will steam, not brown, and the pan juices will burn.

Butter heated to the smoking point will usually burn but, if it is combined with vegetable oil (half and half), it can be heated to the necessary high temperature for sautéing. Clarified butter (page 35) is also used for sautéing because in the clarification process the milk particles have been removed and the butter burns less easily.

Scald. This actually means to heat milk or cream just to, but not above, the boiling point or until a film shines or wrinkles over the surface. For safety's sake, many cooks prefer to heat the milk or cream over hot water rather than run the risk, over direct heat, of its "catching" on the bottom of the pan.

Sieve. Many recipes in the book call for a fine sieve. By fine, Jacques and Helen mean very, very fine indeed—the equivalent of several layers of cheesecloth (which you can use as an alternative). It should also be large enough to do the job, not tea-strainer size.

Simmer. To simmer means to cook in water which is maintained at a fairly steady temperature between 185° and 205° F., or just below boiling. The best way to be sure of the temperature is to use a thermometer (a candy or frying thermometer). When liquids are heated to this temperature, bubbles form slowly and collapse below the surface of the liquid. The water sort of shivers. (The French expression for simmering is to make the water shiver or *frémir.*) When the bubbles break on the surface, simmering ends and boiling begins. To poach, *pocher,* means to cook in simmering liquid.

Spatula. There are wooden and rubber spatulas. The former, flat and sturdy, is best for stirring heavy mixtures. A rubber spatula—which should have a wood handle (it won't break or melt) rather than plastic—is excellent for blending or folding light mixtures.

Thermometer. The two thermometers these cooks consider essential are a meat thermometer and a candy or frying thermometer. The latter is used to test the temperature of any liquid mixture cooked on top of the stove or the fat in which foods are deep fried.

Tomates Concassées. This is the French version of stewed tomatoes. Peel and seed 4 tomatoes, then dice them. Melt 2 tablespoons butter in a saucepan. When it is hot, add the diced tomatoes and a sprinkle of salt. Simmer very slowly for 20 minutes, stirring occasionally.

Tomatoes, to Peel and Seed. Cut out the stem ends of ripe tomatoes, then cover the tomatoes with boiling water and let stand for 15 to 20 seconds; unripe tomatoes may take a few seconds longer. Plunge into cold water. Then, with a small sharp knife, start peeling at the stem end. To seed, cut a slice off the stem end or cut the tomato crosswise into halves; squeeze gently to extract seeds.

Tomato Sauce. In a saucepan heat 3 tablespoons olive oil. Add

1 small finely chopped onion, 1 small minced garlic clove, and 1 cup minced celery. Sauté until the vegetables are tender but not browned. Add 2 cups canned Italian plum tomatoes and simmer for 15 minutes. Stir in 3 tablespoons tomato paste and cook for 20 minutes longer. At this point if the sauce is not liquid enough, stir in ½ cup of beef or chicken broth. Season with salt, freshly ground white pepper, and a pinch of orégano. Serve with any dish that calls for a good tomato sauce.

Unmolding Hot Dishes. (See Aspic for unmolding cold dishes.) Molds of hot food are usually oiled or greased before the food is put in to make unmolding easier. Place a serving platter upside down on top of the mold, hold mold and platter tightly together, and invert.

Velouté, Sauce Velouté. This sauce is made in exactly the same ways as sauce Béchamel (page 33), but instead of milk the liquid used is chicken, veal, or fish stock.

PART II

Extra Yolks in ~ ~ ~

Cocktail Fare

Soups

Entrées

Vegetables

Sauces

Desserts

Extra Yolks in ~ ~ ~
Cocktail Fare

BEURRE AUX JAUNES
(Butter and Yolks for Canapés)

~ 4 egg yolks
½ pound sweet butter, softened
Salt
Freshly ground white pepper
Cayenne (optional)

Place the yolks in a cup or ramekin, then cook, covered, in a pan of simmering water for 15 to 20 minutes, until hard. When cool, push through a fine sieve, or blend in the electric blender, until you have a very fine and homogeneous purée.

Beat or work the butter until creamy, then combine it thoroughly with the yolk purée. Season highly with salt, pepper and cayenne.

Beurre aux jaunes is used for decorating canapés with a tube, or as a spread on bread for canapés or sandwiches. Makes about 1¼ cups.

FRIED CHEESE FINGERS

∞ 2 egg yolks
½ cup grated cheese*
Cream
Firm day-old bread
Butter

Beat the yolks until light, then combine with the cheese, adding enough cream to make a spreadable paste.

Cut crusts off sliced bread and cut each slice into 3 fingers. Spread one side with the cheese mixture. Sauté, *un*spread side down, in hot butter only until lightly browned. Baste a few times with the butter in the pan.

* Any cheese may be used.

TWO-CHEESE STRAWS

1½ cups all-purpose flour
½ teaspoon salt
½ teaspoon white pepper
Good dash of cayenne
¼ pound butter
⅓ cup packed down finely grated Swiss
and Parmesan cheese, half and half
∞ 1 egg yolk beaten with 1 tablespoon water

Line a baking sheet with brown paper and set aside. Mix the flour, salt, pepper and cayenne together. Rub the butter into the mixture with your hands, then work in the cheeses, mixing well. Stir in the beaten yolk with a fork. Then knead briefly with the heel of your hand.

Roll the dough out about ¼ inch thick on a lightly floured board. With a sharp knife, cut the pastry into strips 2 to 3 inches long and about ¼ inch wide. Use a ruler to guide you.

Place on the prepared baking sheet and bake in a preheated 400° F. oven for about 10 minutes, or until golden. Lift from the baking sheet immediately with a spatula and cool on a wire rack. Makes about 48.

COCKTAIL CODFISH BALLS

> 1 package (2 ounces) shredded salt cod
> ½ cup heavy cream
> 1½ cups water
> 2 large Idaho or 3 California "long white" potatoes, baked
> 2 egg yolks
> Freshly ground white pepper
> Dash of ground ginger
> Fine fresh bread crumbs
> Oil for deep frying

Prepare the codfish according to the directions on the package. Set aside. Heat the cream with the water to the boiling point. Take off the heat and whip in briskly the smoothly puréed potatoes. Combine thoroughly with the drained codfish. Mix in the yolks, pepper to taste (pepper is unusually good with cod), and the ginger. Taste here for salt. How much, if any, depends on the saltiness of the codfish. Refrigerate the mixture until cool.

When cold shape into balls about the size of walnuts, roll in bread crumbs, and refrigerate for at least 30 minutes. Makes about 30 balls.

At serving time, heat the oil to 400° F. on a thermometer. Fry the codfish balls, a few at a time, in the hot oil until brown and crusty all over, a matter of minutes. Drain on paper towels.

Serve piping hot in napkin-lined dish with Tomato Sauce (see Glossary) for dipping.

Extra Yolks in ~ ~ ~
Soups

GRATINÉE LYONNAISE AU PORTO
(Onion Soup Lyonnaise Style)

2 tablespoons butter
1 large onion, sliced very thin
3 cups beef or chicken broth
Salt
Freshly ground white pepper
4 slices of firm-textured bread, toasted
¾ cup grated Gruyère cheese
3 egg yolks
¾ cup port wine

Melt the butter in a generous saucepan, add the sliced onion, and sauté for 10 to 15 minutes, or until light brown. Add the broth and salt and pepper to taste, and bring to a boil; cook for 10 minutes.

Meanwhile, cut each slice of toasted bread into 8 squares. Place one third of the toast squares in the bottom of a soup tureen (any capacious, ovenproof casserole handsome enough to go to the table will do). Sprinkle with some of the cheese, add more toast, then more cheese, saving enough to sprinkle over the top of the soup. Fill the tureen with the hot soup, with the remaining cheese on top. Place in a 400°F. oven for 25 minutes.

Bring the *gratinée* to the table. In front of the guests, combine the yolks with the wine in a deep soup plate, and whip very hard with a fork. With a ladle make a "hole" in the *gratinée,* pour in the port mixture, and fold into the soup with the ladle. Serves 4 or 6.

This soup, specifically from the Lyonnais region, is a marvelous winter dish that is served in France when you go out at night—"on the town," as Americans say. Around 4 or 5 o'clock in the morning, it is a sort of custom for everybody to eat *la gratinée.*

POTAGE CRÈME DE TOMATES PARISIENNE
(Cream of Tomato Soup)

4 tablespoons sweet butter
½ medium onion, chopped
3 fresh tomatoes, coarsely chopped
½ cup tomato purée
2 tablespoons flour
2½ cups chicken or beef broth
Salt
Freshly ground white pepper
Dash of sugar
∽ 3 egg yolks
¾ cup light cream

Heat 2 tablespoons of the butter in a saucepan. Add the onion and sauté for 5 minutes, or until lightly browned. Add the tomatoes and tomato purée and cook for 2 minutes. Mix in the flour and cook for 2 more minutes, giving mixture an occasional stir. Add the broth (if served on a fast day, replace broth with water) and bring to a boil. Season to taste with salt and pepper and the sugar. Then simmer for 15 minutes. Strain,* or blend in an electric blender for 30 seconds.

Make the *liaison* with the egg yolks and cream and combine with the soup at once (see Glossary), or combine with the hot soup just before serving. If at once, the soup must be kept hot over hot, not boiling, water, otherwise it may curdle.

At the very last minute, stir in the remaining butter, bit by bit, with a large wooden spoon. Serves 6.

* The way Jacques strains the soup, with professional equipment, gives a better texture, but the blender is a good substitute.

POTAGE GERMINY
(*Cream of Sorrel Soup*)

This is a very delicate and "involving" soup to make, Jacques says, calling for skill and patience. He suggests that if you "miss it the first time," you should not be too disappointed but try your hand again.

1 small bunch of fresh sorrel
1 tablespoon chopped fresh chervil
2 tablespoons butter
4 egg yolks
1 cup heavy cream
3 cups beef or chicken broth, heated
1 tablespoon arrowroot
Salt
Freshly ground white pepper
Croutons (see Glossary)

Slice the sorrel into very fine julienne to make about ½ cup, and add the chervil. Melt the butter in a heavy pan, add the greens, and cook over medium heat for 10 minutes. Set aside.

Combine yolks and cream in the top of a double boiler and beat together with a whip over simmering water for 10 minutes. This long constant whipping should give you a very creamy *liaison,* light and fluffy in consistency.

Take off the heat and combine the *liaison* with the heated broth (see Glossary), whipping hard. Mix the arrowroot with enough cold water to make a smooth paste. Stir into the soup, and season with salt and pepper. Place back over hot water and cook, stirring constantly with a wooden spatula, until the soup begins to coat the spatula (temperature on a thermometer should not go beyond 175° F.).

Keep warm in a double boiler, over hot, not boiling, water, until serving time. Strain off any surplus juice from the sorrel, and add the sorrel to the soup just before serving. It is really a garnish. Or chill in the refrigerator after adding the sorrel and serve cold. It is delicious either way. Serve with croutons only if hot. Serves 6.

BILLI-BI SOUP

6 pounds mussels (about 6 dozen)
1 cup dry white wine
1 medium-sized onion, diced
2 tablespoons chopped parsley
Dash of dried thyme
1 bay leaf
Freshly ground white pepper
2 cups heavy cream
3 egg yolks
2 tablespoons chopped chives

Place the well-scrubbed mussels (see Glossary), the wine, onion, parsley, thyme, bay leaf, and pepper to taste in a very large kettle (not aluminum). Bring to a boil, cover, and cook for 5 to 10 minutes over high heat, or until all the mussels have opened. Discard any mussels that do not open.

To move the mussels from one level to another while they cook, lift the kettle occasionally with both hands, holding the cover with your thumbs, and toss in an up-and-down motion. If you can't manage this alone, then stir frequently with a long wooden spoon. The objective, as must be apparent, is to have all the mussels cook at one time. At the end of this cooking period, add 1½ cups of the cream to the kettle and bring to a rolling boil over high heat. At this point, lift the mussels out of the broth with a slotted spoon or tongs and set aside.

Strain the broth through a very fine sieve or several layers of cheesecloth into another pan (not aluminum). Make a *liaison* with the remaining cream and the yolks and combine with the strained broth. Heat, stirring constantly with a wooden spoon,

over low heat until soup has thickened slightly. Do not allow it
to boil. Take off the heat and allow soup to stand long enough so
that if there should be any sand lurking around, it will settle to
the bottom. Pour into a bowl slowly, watching carefully for any
signs of sediment. Taste for seasoning. Refrigerate.

Billi-Bi is customarily served cold with a sprinkling of minced
fresh chives, but it is very good hot, too. Serves 6.

NOTE: The cooked mussels, which are not served in the soup,
can be served cold as a first course for luncheon or dinner.
Remove from shells and mix with 1 cup Sauce Gribiche
(page 95).

Or, place the cooked mussels, out of the shell, in a dish,
add 1 small onion sliced very thin, a generous sprinkling of
minced parsley, enough vinegar and oil (1 to 3) to cover,
and salt and pepper to taste. Cover tightly and refrigerate. It,
too, makes a good first course. Serve with French bread.

CRÈME DE VOLAILLE AUX CROÛTONS
(Cream of Chicken Soup with Croutons)

1 cup light cream
3½ cups Sauce Velouté*
3 egg yolks
2 tablespoons sweet butter
Croutons (see Glossary)

Stir ½ cup of the cream into the sauce velouté, and bring to a boil.
Take off the heat and strain through a fine sieve or several layers

*Make the Sauce Velouté (see Glossary) in these proportions: 6
tablespoons sweet butter, 6 tablespoons flour, 2⅔ cups canned condensed
chicken broth.

of cheesecloth. Make a *liaison* with the remaining cream and the egg yolks in a bowl and beat very hard.

Just before serving, combine the *liaison* with the soup (see Glossary), stirring very fast. Then add the butter, bit by bit, stirring steadily with a big wooden spoon. Serve piping hot with croutons (see Glossary). Serves 6.

GAZPACHO

> 1 cucumber
> 2 large ripe tomatoes
> 1 large green pepper
> 1 small onion
> ⅓ cup tomato purée
> 1 tablespoon white vinegar or tarragon
> 2 tablespoons olive oil
> ½ garlic clove
> ~ 3 egg yolks
> ¾ cup cold water
> Salt
> Freshly ground white pepper
> Cayenne
> Croutons (see Glossary)

To prepare the garnish, cut off about one third of the cucumber, of each tomato, and of the green pepper. Cut each one separately into very small dice, place in small individual bowls, and refrigerate.

Chop the remainder of the vegetables and the onion coarsely. Place with the tomato purée, vinegar, olive oil, garlic, egg yolks and the water in the container of an electric blender. Blend for 1 minute. Pour into a bowl; season with salt, pepper and cayenne to taste. Chill in the refrigerator.

At serving time, fill chilled soup bowls with the cold gazpacho and pass the vegetable garnish and the croutons separately. Serves 6.

CALCUTTA CREAM SOUP

2 tablespoons butter
1 medium onion, chopped
¾ tablespoon authoritative curry powder
½ apple, chopped
¼ cup flour
3 cups chicken or beef broth
Salt
Freshly ground white pepper
1 cup milk
½ cup light cream
3 egg yolks

Melt the butter in a heavy saucepan, add the onion, and sauté for 5 minutes. Stir in the curry powder and apple and cook for 1 minute. Stir in the flour. Add the broth gradually, stirring constantly. Bring to a boil, still stirring, and allow to cook, over moderate heat, for 10 minutes. Season to taste with salt and pepper. Add the milk and bring to a boil again.

Beat the cream and egg yolks together. Combine this *liaison* (see Glossary) with the soup just before serving. Serve piping hot. Serves 6.

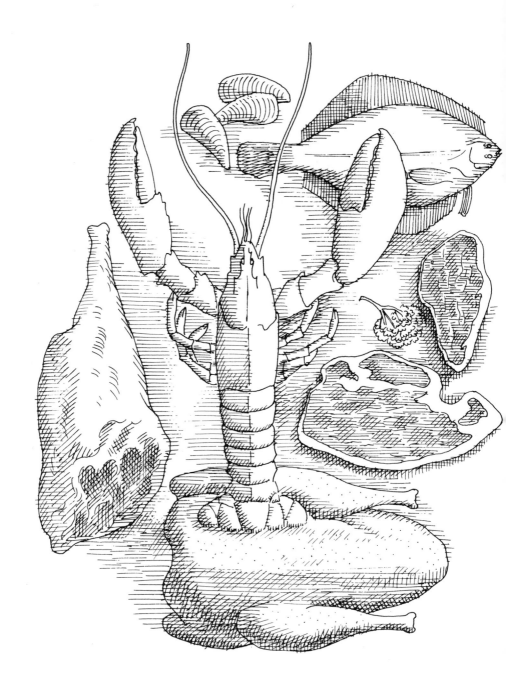

Extra Yolks in ~ ~ ~
Entrées

GNOCCHI ROMAINE

> 1 quart milk
> Salt
> Freshly ground white pepper
> Dash of grated nutmeg
> ¾ cup farina* or semolina
> 4 tablespoons butter
> 4 egg yolks
> 1 cup freshly grated Swiss cheese
> 1 cup heavy cream (about)

Line a flat baking dish with wax paper and set aside.

Combine the milk, salt to taste, pepper (several grinds of the mill), and nutmeg in a saucepan. Bring to a boil, add the farina, and cook, stirring constantly with a wooden spatula, for about 5 minutes, until cooked. The mixture should be very thick and look like a heavy dough.

---

* Farina cooks faster and is easier to find than semolina. It doesn't make a great difference in the final taste which you use.

Take off the heat and beat in half of the butter, then the egg yolks, one at a time, beating very rapidly. Pour into the prepared pan, 1½ to 2 inches deep, and smooth with a spatula. Cool.

When cold, cut into shapes with a cookie cutter, or into squares or oblongs, in short, whatever you like. Brush both sides of the "shaped" gnocchi with remaining butter, melted. Arrange in a baking dish, cover with the grated cheese, and bake in a pre-heated 425° F. oven until gnocchi start to brown. Then spoon 1 tablespoon cream over each piece. Return to oven until golden. Serves 6.

LOBSTER NEWBURG

6 tablespoons butter
3 cups large pieces of cooked lobster meat
⅓ cup Cognac
2 cups heavy cream
∾ 6 egg yolks, slightly beaten
Salt
Cayenne
6 patty shells, heated

Melt the butter in a large heavy saucepan, add the lobster, and sauté over high heat for 5 minutes.

Heat the Cognac, ignite, and pour over the lobster. Stir in the cream and bring to a boil. Spoon a couple of tablespoons of the hot sauce into the yolks, whipping briskly with a wire whip. Pour back into the lobster mixture and cook, stirring constantly, over an extremely low heat, or better, in a double boiler, until sauce has thickened slightly. Season to taste with salt and cayenne. The sauce should not, correctly, be heavy but rather light. Whatever happens, don't allow it to boil or it's likely to curdle.

Spoon into heated patty shells. Serves 6.

MOULES À LA POULETTE
(Mussels in Cream Sauce)

> 10 pounds mussels (about 10 dozen)
> 2 medium-sized onions, diced
> 1 garlic clove, chopped
> 5 tablespoons coarsely chopped parsley
> Dash of dried thyme
> 1 bay leaf
> Freshly ground white pepper
> 2 cups dry white wine
> ¼ pound butter
> 3 tablespoons flour
> 1 cup heavy cream
> ~ 3 egg yolks

Put the cleaned mussels (see Glossary) in a big kettle (not aluminum) with the onions, garlic, 3 tablespoons of the parsley, the thyme, bay leaf, pepper to taste, the wine and 5 tablespoons of the butter. Cover tightly and cook over high heat for 5 to 10 minutes, or until all the mussels have opened. Discard any that do not open.

So mussels on top can benefit by the broth in which they are steaming, and so all will be cooked at the same time, occasionally shake the kettle in an up-and-down motion to move them from one level to another. This is best accomplished by lifting the kettle with both hands, your thumbs holding the cover, and tossing the mussels. (You may need a strong arm to help you.)

Lift the mussels from the broth and transfer them to a large, broad and deep earthenware casserole or tureen. Break the mussels apart, keeping only the shells containing the mussels. Set aside and keep warm. Strain the broth into a clean pan (not aluminum), leaving a small residue in the bottom just in case some of the sand eluded you in cleaning.

Make a *beurre manié* (page 37) with remaining butter and the flour. Add to the broth, bit by bit, whipping constantly with a wire whip until smooth. Bring to a boil, reduce heat, and cook for 8 to 10 minutes. Add ½ cup of the cream, bring to a boil again, then take off the heat.

Meanwhile, make a *liaison* (see Glossary) with the remaining cream and the egg yolks. Combine with the sauce. Return to the heat and bring to a boil but do not boil. Pour over mussels and sprinkle with remainder of the chopped parsley. Serves 6.

FILETS DE SOLE DUGLÉRÉ
(Sole Fillets with Tomatoes)

> 7 tablespoons butter
> Salt
> Freshly ground white pepper
> ½ cup chopped shallots or green onion bulbs
> 12 fillets of sole (about 1½ pounds)
> 2 large ripe tomatoes, peeled, seeded and chopped
> 3 tablespoons chopped parsley
> 1½ cups dry white wine
> 1 cup water
> 4 tablespoons flour
> 1 cup heavy or light cream
> ∽ 3 egg yolks
> 2 tablespoons Cognac

Butter a heavy shallow baking pan, sprinkle with salt and pepper, and scatter 6 tablespoons of the shallots over the bottom. Line up the fillets, rolled or folded in two, on top. Scatter remaining shallots over the fish and sprinkle with salt and pepper. Add the tomatoes, 2 tablespoons of the parsley, and the wine mixed with the water.

Butter a piece of wax paper large enough to cover the pan and place it, buttered side down, flat on top. Bring the liquid to a boil over high heat. Take the pan off the heat and place in a preheated 400° F. oven for 10 to 12 minutes, or until a fork pierces the flesh of the fish easily. Remove from the oven. Arrange the fillets on a buttered serving platter, cover again with the buttered wax paper, and keep warm.

Pour the broth into a clean saucepan and reduce to two thirds. Make a *beurre manié* with 3 tablespoons of the butter and the flour (page 37). Add to the broth, bit by bit, and cook, whipping constantly, for 10 minutes.

Add ¾ cup of the cream and bring to a boil. Take off the heat. Beat the egg yolks and remaining cream together in a bowl, then little by little combine this *liaison* (see Glossary) with the hot broth. Add the Cognac and remaining butter, whipping vigorously. Pour sauce over fillets and sprinkle with the rest of the parsley. Serves 6.

LEMON CHICKEN

1 chicken (3½ to 4 pounds)
1 onion stuck with 2 cloves
2 celery stalks with tops
1 carrot
Several parsley sprigs
2 teaspoons salt
Few peppercorns, crushed
1 thick slice of lemon
Peel from 1 lemon, slivered and blanched
Juice of 1 lemon
¼ cup dry sherry
1 cup heavy cream
2 egg yolks

Place the chicken with the onion, celery, carrot, parsley, salt, peppercorns and the slice of lemon in a large heavy kettle. Add enough water to cover the chicken. Place over a low heat and bring to a boil slowly. Cover, then simmer for approximately 1¼ hours, until chicken is tender when pierced with a fork. Another test: when the skin begins to shrink from the ends of the leg bones and the bones move easily in their sockets, the chicken is perfectly cooked. Cool the chicken right in the stock. This takes quite some time, so it is best done in the refrigerator overnight.

Remove the cold chicken from the broth, pull off all the meat in large pieces, and discard the skin, fat and gristle. Toss the carcass and bones back into the broth, bring to a boil over a high heat, and boil until sauce has reduced to about 2 cups. Strain through a fine sieve or several layers of cheesecloth wrung out in cold water. Place back over the heat, add the slivered lemon peel, lemon juice and sherry. Cook for 5 minutes. Then taste for seasoning; it may need a "hair" of salt.

Meanwhile, cut the chicken meat into long slender pieces, actually, julienne.

Make a *liaison* (see Glossary) with the cream and yolks. Combine with the broth and cook very slowly, whipping constantly, until the sauce thickens slightly. Arrange the chicken pieces in a proper serving dish (oblong would be nice), pour the lemon sauce over it, and refrigerate. Serve very cold. Serves 4 or 5.

CHICKEN HASH

3 cups pieces of cooked chicken breast, minced
1½ cups light cream
¾ cups Sauce Béchamel*
1 cup milk
3 tablespoons butter
2 tablespoons flour
1 medium onion, sliced
¼ teaspoon salt
~ 3 egg yolks
3 tablespoons grated Parmesan cheese
1 package (10 ounces) frozen peas (*petits pois*)

64

Combine the minced chicken and the cream in a heavy saucepan and cook over low heat until the cream has been reduced to about half of the original amount. Combine the sauce Béchamel with the chicken mixture, pour all into a shallow baking dish, and keep hot.

Bring the milk to a boil, but do not boil. Take off the heat and skim the film, if any, from the surface. Melt 2 tablespoons of the butter in a saucepan and stir in the flour until smooth. Cook for a couple of minutes. Gradually add the hot milk, stirring constantly with a wire whip. Add the sliced onion and the salt and cook over low heat for about 15 minutes, stirring frequently.

Beat the yolks slightly, add a few tablespoons of the hot sauce to them, then combine the two, whipping vigorously with a whip. Stir in remaining butter and last of all the cheese with a spatula. Spoon this sauce over the chicken, and slide the baking dish under a preheated broiler 4 to 5 inches from the broiling unit, just long enough for the sauce to become flecked with gold.

Meanwhile, cook the frozen peas according to package directions. Drain thoroughly and purée in an electric blender. Season with salt and freshly ground pepper. Place the purée in a pastry bag fitted with a fluted tube and pipe a border of the puréed peas all around the edge of the baking dish. Serves 4.

* Make the Sauce Béchamel (see Glossary) in these proportions: $1\frac{1}{2}$ tablespoons butter, $1\frac{1}{2}$ tablespoons flour, $\frac{3}{4}$ cup milk, seasoned with salt and freshly ground white pepper.

FRICASSÉE DE POULET VALLÉE D'AUGE
(Normandy Chicken Fricassee)

        1 frying chicken (3 pounds), cut up, or
          3 halves of frying chicken, each cut into
          2 pieces
    Salt
    Freshly ground white pepper
    5 tablespoons butter
    3 tablespoons vegetable oil
    1 cup diced carrots
    2 medium onions, diced
    2 garlic cloves, chopped
    ¼ cup diced celery
    2 tablespoons coarsely chopped parsley
    Dash of dried thyme
    1 bay leaf
    ¾ cup dry white wine
    2½ cups water
    2 tablespoons flour
    1 cup light cream
∽   2 egg yolks
    ½ cup cooked peas, heated

Sprinkle the chicken pieces with salt and pepper. Heat 3 tablespoons of the butter and all of the oil in a large heavy shallow pan.
When hot, add the chicken pieces, a few at a time—do not crowd
the pan. Reduce heat and cook for 5 minutes, turning the pieces
once or twice. Do not allow them to take on color. Add the carrots,
onions, garlic, celery, parsley, thyme, bay leaf, and a sprinkling of
salt and white pepper. Cover and simmer for 5 minutes, turning
the vegetables over once or twice. Add the wine and water. Cover
and simmer for 20 minutes, or until chicken is tender when pierced
with a fork.

Knead the remaining butter with the flour to make a *beurre
manié* (page 37); beat the cream and yolks together. Set aside.

Lift the cooked chicken from the pan with a fork and arrange on a hot serving platter (you can, at this point, remove the bones, but it's not necessary). Add the *beurre manié* bit by bit to the broth, whipping steadily with a wire whip until smooth. Bring to a boil, reduce heat, and simmer for 8 to 10 minutes. Just before serving, combine with the cream and yolk *liaison* (see Glossary), whipping vigorously. Take off the heat, stir in half of the peas, and taste for seasoning.

To serve, pour the sauce over the chicken pieces and scatter remaining peas on top. Serves 6.

POULET À LA CRÈME BRESSANE
(*Chicken in Cream*)

> ½ cup flour
> Salt
> Freshly ground white pepper
> 1 chicken (3 pounds), cut up for stewing, or
> 3 halves of frying chickens, each cut into
>   2 pieces
> 4 tablespoons butter, in all
> 1 medium onion, cut into halves
> 1 bay leaf
> 2 tablespoons chopped parsley
> Dash of ground thyme
> ¾ cup dry white wine
> 2½ cups water
> 2 egg yolks
> 1 cup light cream

Season the flour with salt and pepper and place the mixture in a paper bag. Add the pieces of chicken, one at a time, and shake to coat well with the flour mixture.

Melt 3 tablespoons of butter in a large shallow heavy skillet (it should be generous enough so chicken pieces can lie flat).

When the butter is foaming, add the chicken pieces and cook on both sides for 10 to 12 minutes, until a nice light gold. Add onion, bay leaf, parsley, thyme, wine and water. Cover, bring to a boil, then reduce heat, and simmer for 25 minutes. In the meantime, make a *beurre manié* (page 37) with remaining butter and 1 tablespoon of flour. Beat the egg yolks together with the cream to make a *liaison*.

Place the cooked chicken on a warm serving platter and keep warm. Add the *beurre manié* to the broth in the pan, nut by nut, whipping constantly with a wire whip. Bring to a boil, then reduce heat to moderate, and cook for 10 to 12 minutes. Combine the *liaison* with the hot broth (see Glossary), whipping constantly. Bring almost up to a boil but do not allow it to boil or chances are it will curdle. Take off the heat. Strain through a fine sieve or several layers of cheesecloth into the top of a double boiler and keep warm over hot water.

At serving time, pour the sauce over the pieces of chicken. Serves 4.

STUFFED DUCK BORDELAISE

1 tablespoon butter
1 medium onion, chopped
2 garlic cloves, chopped
The duck liver, chopped
⅓ cup chopped mushrooms
1 pound pork sausage meat
Dash of salt
Dash of freshly ground white pepper
Dash of ground thyme
4 slices of firm bread
1 cup milk
∞ 4 egg yolks
½ cup coarsely chopped black olives
2 tablespoons chopped parsley
1 duck (5 pounds)

Melt the butter in a heavy pan, add the onion, and sauté for 3 minutes; add the garlic and sauté for 1 minute; add the liver and mushrooms and sauté for 1 minute, stirring constantly. Mix in the pork sausage and seasonings and cook, still stirring, for about 5 minutes, or until pork has lost its color.

Mash the bread into the milk, add the egg yolks, and work together until you have a smooth paste.

Take the sausage mixture off the heat and cool in the refrigerator for 10 minutes. Then stir in the bread mixture, the olives and parsley. Cool until stuffing can be handled. Stuff the duck, sew or skewer the opening, and truss securely to keep the bird shapely. Rub the skin with salt and pepper.

Place the duck on its back on a rack in a roasting pan and roast in a preheated 400° F. oven for about 20 minutes. Turn to one side and continue roasting for 20 to 25 minutes, then turn on the other side and roast for the same length of time. When nicely browned, turn again on its back, reduce oven heat to 375° F. and finish cooking. This will take about 2 hours in all.

About 45 minutes before the duck has finished roasting, drain off three fourths of the fat and add 1½ cups of water to pan.

Serve the stuffed duck with its juices and *Petits Pois à l'Étuvée* (page 80). Serves 4 or 5.

ÉMINCÉ DE VOLAILLE ALSACIENNE
(Alsatian Chicken and Noodles)

> 3 halves of frying chickens (1¼ pounds each
>   half)
> 1 medium onion
> 1 carrot
> 1 bay leaf
> Dash of ground thyme
> Salt
> 3 or 4 peppercorns, crushed
> Few parsley sprigs
> 3 cups cold water
> 6 tablespoons butter
> 4 tablespoons flour
> 1 cup light cream
> ∽ 3 egg yolks
> Tomates Concassées (made with 1 large or
>   2 small tomatoes; see Glossary)
> 1 pound noodles, cooked

Place the chicken halves in a large heavy deep pan with the onion, carrot, bay leaf, thyme, salt to taste, the peppercorns, parsley and water. Bring to a boil slowly, then simmer, covered, for about 45 minutes, or until tender.

Remove the chicken from the broth. When cool enough to handle, bone, then slice the meat into long thin pieces. Place on a warm platter, cover with foil, and keep warm.

Meanwhile, work 4 tablespoons of the butter into the flour to make a *beurre manié* (page 37). Add to broth (you should have about 2 cups), bit by bit, whipping constantly. When thoroughly combined, cook for 10 minutes, stirring often.

Beat the cream and egg yolks together; combine the *liaison* with the broth (see Glossary), whipping vigorously. Strain the sauce into the top of a double boiler and keep warm over hot water.

Make the Tomates Concassées. Season with white pepper.

Melt remaining butter in a saucepan; add the cooked noodles and a pinch of salt. Sauté for a few minutes.

At serving time, place some noodles on each person's plate; arrange slices of chicken on top. Spoon 3 or 4 tablespoons of the sauce over the chicken with a tablespoon or so of the tomatoes on top. Serves 6.

BLANQUETTE DE VEAU À L'ANCIENNE
(*Veal Blanquette*)

4 pounds veal chuck or shoulder, cut into
   3-inch cubes
2 quarts cold water
1 very large onion, halved
3 garlic cloves, unpeeled
½ teaspoon peppercorns, crushed
1 large carrot, scraped
3 tablespoons chopped parsley root*
1 large pinch of dried thyme
1 bay leaf
1¼ teaspoons salt
¼ pound butter
1 cup flour
1½ cups light or heavy cream
3 egg yolks
¼ pound fresh mushrooms, sliced, or
   2 cans (4 ounces each) drained
¾ cup sliced dill pickles or small French
   sour pickles

* If parsley root is not available, use a good bunch of fresh parsley.

Blanch the meat in boiling water for 5 minutes. Refresh or rinse in cold water and drain. Place in a large heavy kettle (not aluminum) with the water, onion, garlic, peppercorns, carrot, parsley root, thyme, bay leaf, and salt. Bring to a rolling boil, then reduce heat and simmer, covered, for 65 minutes, or until meat is tender when tested with a fork. Lift the cooked meat out of the broth. Set aside and keep warm.

Meanwhile, make a *beurre manié* with 7 tablespoons of the butter and the flour (page 37). Strain the broth through a fine sieve or several layers of cheesecloth into a clean kettle. Add the *beurre manié,* bit by bit, whipping fast with a wire whip. Bring to a boil, reduce heat, and simmer for 20 minutes.

Make a *liaison* with the cream and egg yolks and combine with the broth (see Glossary), whipping vigorously and steadily until smooth. Strain over the meat.

Melt the remaining tablespoon of butter and sauté the fresh mushrooms for 2 or 3 minutes. Just drain the canned ones. Add the mushrooms to the stew. Put the stew back over heat and bring to a boil again, but do not cook further. Keep hot over, but not in, simmering water until serving time. Just before serving, stir in the chopped pickles. Serves 8.

~   NOTE: For a different and unusual Veal Blanquette, see page 180.

CÔTES DE VEAU À LA CRÈME
(Veal Chops in Cream)

6 veal chops (about 6 ounces each)
Salt
Pepper
Flour
4 tablespoons butter
2 tablespoons vegetable oil
1 tablespoon chopped shallots or green
  onion bulbs
2 cups sliced fresh mushrooms
1 cup light cream
2 tablespoons Cognac
2 egg yolks

Sprinkle the chops with salt and pepper, then dip both sides into flour to coat well, shaking off any excess.

Combine 3 tablespoons of the butter with the oil in a large heavy skillet. When foaming, add the chops and reduce the heat. Cook on one side for about 8 minutes—they should be golden brown—turn, and cook on the other side until golden. Cover and cook over low heat for 3 to 5 minutes. At this point the chops should be cooked, moist, and so tender you can cut them with a fork. Arrange on a warm serving platter.

Add the shallots to the same pan and cook for 1 or 2 minutes over high heat. Add the mushrooms and cook, covered, for 5 minutes; add ½ cup of the cream and bring to a boil.

Meanwhile, make a *beurre manié* (page 37) with the remaining tablespoon of butter and 1 tablespoon of flour. Add to the sauce, a nut at a time, whipping constantly until smooth. Bring to a boil, then simmer for 2 or 3 minutes. Stir in the Cognac.

Beat the egg yolks into the remaining cream to make a *liaison* (see Glossary) and combine with the sauce, whipping constantly with a whip.

Pour sauce over chops and serve piping hot with boiled potatoes and young green beans. Serves 6.

MOUSSAKA D'AGNEAU AUX COURGETTES
(Moussaka with Zucchini)

Moussaka is always made with lamb, often leftover leg of lamb or even lamb stew meat, and usually with eggplant. In this version zucchini replaces the eggplant, making a very good and interesting recipe.

> 3 large zucchini (about ¾ pound each)
> Salt
> Freshly ground white pepper
> 1 cup flour
> 1 cup vegetable oil
> 2 medium onions, coarsely chopped
> 3 garlic cloves, chopped
> ½ pound mushrooms, coarsely chopped
> 2 cups chopped cooked lamb
> ⅓ cup tomato purée
> ∽ 3 egg yolks
> 1 can (10¾ ounces) brown gravy
> Tomates Concassées (made with 4 tomatoes; see Glossary)
> Parsley

Wash the zucchini, but do not peel them, and cut off both ends. Take half of one zucchini and chop coarsely. To make large pieces (necessary, as you will see, to finish the dish), cut remaining zucchini on the bias into long slices about ½ inch thick. This will leave you with 5 short pieces which should be coarsely chopped and added to the other chopped zucchini.

Sprinkle the slices with salt and pepper, and coat with flour, shaking off any excess. Sauté in ¾ cup of the oil until lightly browned on both sides. Set aside.

Heat the remaining oil in a skillet and sauté the onion in it for 5 minutes. Add the garlic and cook for 1 minute. Add the chopped zucchini and mushrooms. Cook, stirring constantly, for 3 more minutes. Next add the lamb. Cook for 3 to 4 minutes longer, stirring with a wooden spatula. Add the tomato purée. Beat the egg yolks with 1 cup of the brown gravy to make a *liaison*. Mix this into the meat mixture gradually, stirring briskly with a wooden spatula. Continue to cook, stirring constantly, for 5 to 6 minutes longer.

Line the sides of a shallow (3 to 4 inches deep) ovenproof baking dish, preferably oval, with the zucchini slices, allowing them to hang over the edge. Spoon the meat and vegetable mixture into the dish, then fold the zucchini slices back over the meat. Cover the top with remaining slices.

About 1½ hours before dinner, place the dish in a preheated 400° F. oven and bake for 40 to 50 minutes. Remove from oven and allow to stand for 15 to 20 minutes. Then turn out onto a warm serving platter.

While the moussaka is baking, make up the *tomates concassées*. Set aside ½ cup of these tomatoes. To the remaining tomatoes, add the remainder of the beef gravy. Bring to a boil, then reduce heat and simmer this sauce for 5 minutes.

Spoon the sauce all around the unmolded moussaka. Place the reserved tomatoes in a bouquet on top, and tuck a little bunch of parsley in the center. Serves 8.

STEAK MARCHAND DE VINS

> 6 steaks (8 to 10 ounces each)
> Salt
> Freshly ground pepper
> 3 tablespoons butter
> 3 tablespoons chopped shallots or green
> onion bulbs
> ¾ cup dry red Burgundy
> 1 cup brown gravy*
> 〜 2 egg yolks

Sprinkle both sides of the steaks with salt and pepper.

Place the butter in a large heavy skillet over high heat. When foaming, add the steaks (as many as the pan will accommodate without crowding) and cook to your taste. Generally, for guests, it is preferable to serve them medium rare. Place cooked steaks on a warm serving platter and keep warm.

Add the shallots to the fat in the pan and sauté for 1 minute over high heat; add the wine and reduce to half. Stir in half of the brown gravy and bring to a boil. Taste for seasoning.

Beat remaining brown gravy together with egg yolks. Combine the *liaison* with the wine mixture (see Glossary), whipping constantly. Bring to a boil and strain over the steaks through a fine sieve. Serve at once.

---

* Lacking brown gravy, use 1 cup beef broth. Make a *beurre manié* (page 37) with 1 tablespoon butter and 1 tablespoon flour. Heat the broth, then add the *beurre manié* bit by bit, whipping constantly with a wire whip until sauce is smooth and thickened. To give it color, add a few drops of Kitchen Bouquet.

If arrowroot is at hand, you can substitute 1 teaspoon of arrowroot for the *beurre manié*. Mix with a little cold water until smooth, then whip into the broth and cook until slightly thickened, stirring constantly.

Extra Yolks in ~ ~ ~
Vegetables

CHAMPIGNONS FARCIS
(Stuffed Mushrooms)

18 big mushrooms
Salt
2 tablespoons salad oil
2 tablespoons butter
1 medium onion, finely chopped
2 garlic cloves, finely chopped
Dash of ground thyme
Dash of freshly ground pepper
1 large ripe tomato, peeled, seeded and
   chopped
～ 3 egg yolks, well beaten
½ cup freshly ground Swiss and Parmesan
   cheese (half and half)

Break the mushroom caps off stems and place caps, bottom side up, in a skillet. Sprinkle with salt and a mixture of 1 tablespoon of the oil and 1 tablespoon of the butter, melted. Cover and cook over low heat for 10 minutes. Lift the caps from the skillet and lay them, bottom side up, on a clean tray. Refrigerate until cool.

Meanwhile, chop mushroom stems very fine. Add remaining oil and butter to skillet, and sauté the chopped stems with the onion for 3 minutes, stirring constantly with a wooden spoon. Add the garlic, thyme, pepper, and tomato. Bring to a boil, then simmer for about 12 minutes. Then add the egg yolks and cook, stirring constantly, for 1 minute. Take off the heat and cool.

Stuff the mushroom caps with the mixture and sprinkle with the cheese. Bake in a preheated 375° F. oven for 25 to 30 minutes, or until lightly browned. Serve with roast beef, steak or chicken. In fact, anything with which mushrooms are compatible.

The stuffed mushrooms, refrigerated and securely covered, will keep for a couple of days.

POIREAUX AU GRATIN
(Gratin of Leeks)

8 to 10 large leeks
½ pound bacon
1 cup water
Salt
Freshly ground white pepper
Dash of ground thyme
2 tablespoons butter
2 tablespoons flour
1 cup milk
3 egg yolks
½ cup heavy cream
2 tablespoons grated Swiss cheese

Cut the leeks into 2-inch pieces, using only the white and light green. Trim off the roots. Split the pieces into quarters (measured, there should be about 6 cups) and wash very thoroughly to get rid of any sand. Lift them out of the water, rather than draining them, or you may get some of the sand you have washed off.

Cut the bacon into 2-inch pieces and sauté in a frying pan until nicely brown. Add the leeks, water, salt and pepper to taste, and thyme. Cover tightly and cook for 15 to 20 minutes, or long enough so leeks are tender and all the water has evaporated.

Melt the butter in a small saucepan, stir in the flour until smooth, add the milk and cook, whipping constantly with a wire whip, until Béchamel comes to a boil. Continue to cook, stirring occasionally, for 5 minutes. Mix with the leeks carefully. Beat egg yolks and cream together, then combine the *liaison* (see Glossary) with the leeks, stirring constantly with a wooden spatula.

Pour into a shallow ovenproof dish, sprinkle with the cheese, and bake in a preheated 375° F. oven for about 20 minutes, until golden brown. Serves 6.

Leeks, like onions, are delicious with beef or fowl.

PETITS POIS À L'ÉTUVÉE
(Braised Green Peas)

> 4 cups fresh young peas
> ¼ pound butter
> ½ cup water
> 2 teaspoons sugar
> 1 tablespoon minced parsley
> Salt
> Freshly ground white pepper
> ∽ 2 egg yolks, well beaten

Place the peas in a heavy saucepan (not aluminum) with all ingredients except the yolks. Bring to a boil, then reduce heat, and simmer until the peas are tender to the bite. Taste for seasoning. Then, very gradually, stir in the beaten egg yolks and cook, over low heat, stirring constantly, until sauce has thickened. Do not allow it to boil. Serves 6.

POTATO CROQUETTES

> 3 big Idaho potatoes or California "long whites"
> 1 tablespoon butter, softened
> ∽ 6 egg yolks
> Salt
> Dash of grated nutmeg
> 1 cup flour (about)
> 4½ cups vegetable oil
> ¼ cup water
> Freshly ground white pepper
> 5 cups fresh bread crumbs (about 12 slices)

Pare the potatoes and cut into quarters. Cook in boiling salted water, covered, until tender when pierced with the point of a small sharp knife. Drain and dry thoroughly in a very hot oven for 5 or 6 minutes. Put through a ricer or food mill. Then beat in the butter, 3 of the egg yolks slightly beaten, a little salt and the nutmeg with a wooden spatula or an electric beater. Potatoes should be very smooth and without any lumps. Cool to room temperature.

Flour your hands, then shape potato mixture into cylinders and roll in flour.

Beat together ½ cup of the vegetable oil with the remaining egg yolks, the water, and salt and pepper to taste. Dip the potato cylinders into the egg mixture, then coat with bread crumbs. Refrigerate.

At serving time, heat the remaining vegetable oil in a large deep kettle to 375° F. on a thermometer, or until a cube of bread browns in 1 minute. Deep fry croquettes, no more than three at a time, for 2 minutes, or until golden. Drain on paper towels. Keep warm in a 300° F. oven. Serves 6.

~ NOTE: If the potato mixture is not dry enough, the croquettes will be too soft to fry and will burst or crack in the fryer. Should your mixture seem too soft, and this is a matter of judgment, work in about ½ cup flour very thoroughly. Chill well before shaping. Then follow directions.

POTATOES DUCHESSE

> 3 big Idaho potatoes or California "long whites"
> 3 tablespoons butter, softened
> ~ 5 egg yolks, slightly beaten
> Salt
> Dash of grated nutmeg
> 1 cup flour

Bake the potatoes in their jackets, then scoop out the pulp with a spoon. Or pare the potatoes, cut into quarters, and cook in boiling salted water to cover until tender when pierced with the point of a small sharp knife. Drain thoroughly, then place in a very hot oven (450° F.) for 5 or 6 minutes to dry very well.

Put pulp of baked or boiled potatoes through a ricer or push through a sieve; then whip in the butter. Beat in the egg yolks, a little salt and the nutmeg with a wooden spatula or, better, with an electric beater. Potatoes should be very smooth and free of all lumps. Cool to room temperature.

Sprinkle board lightly with flour, and flour your hands. Shape potato mixture into balls, round flat cakes, or little rolls. Then coat lightly with flour. Place on baking sheet and bake in a preheated 425° F. oven until golden.

Use as an accompaniment for meat dishes. This amount will serve 6.

Potatoes Duchesse are also used to garnish the edge of finished dishes. In this case, the potato mixture is put through a pastry tube, then browned the same way—in a hot oven (425° F.).

Extra Yolks in ⁓ ⁓ ⁓
Sauces

SAUCE MORNAY

> 2 cups Sauce Béchamel*
> 3 egg yolks
> ½ cup grated Swiss cheese

Beat the egg yolks into the hot sauce Béchamel, one at a time, stirring very fast and hard with a whip. Fold in the cheese with a spatula at the very last minute, just before serving. Do not use a whip for this operation or the cheese will "string" and the sauce will look like glue.

Sauce Mornay is used to make au gratin potatoes when done in the oven, or to serve with cauliflower, eggs, shellfish, etc. Makes about 3 cups.

* Make the Sauce Béchamel (see Glossary) in these proportions: 4 tablespoons butter, 4 tablespoons flour, 2 cups milk. Season with salt and freshly ground white pepper.

SAUCE ALLEMANDE

> 2 cups Sauce Velouté*
> ½ cup light cream
> 3 egg yolks
> Salt
> Freshly ground white pepper

Make the sauce velouté and set aside for the moment.

* Make the Sauce Velouté (see Glossary) in these proportions: 4 tablespoons butter, 4 tablespoons flour, and 2 cups chicken or beef broth.

Beat the cream and yolks together. Combine this *liaison* (see (Glossary) with the sauce velouté, whipping constantly with a wire whip. Season to taste with salt and pepper. Keep warm in the top of a double boiler. Makes about 3 cups.

Sauce Allemande is customarily served with poached eggs, breast of chicken, and hot vegetables such as asparagus, spinach, cauliflower, etc.

SAUCE BÂTARDE

> 3 tablespoons butter
> 4 tablespoons flour
> 2 cups water
> 3 egg yolks
> ⅓ cup light cream or milk
> Salt
> Freshly ground white pepper
> Juice of ¼ lemon

Make a *roux blanc* by melting the butter in a saucepan (not aluminum) and stirring in the flour (page 38). Cook for a minute or two, then add the water. Bring to a boil and cook for 5 more minutes.

Beat the egg yolks into the cream or milk. Combine this *liaison* (see Glossary) with the first mixture, beating constantly with a wire whip. Season to taste with salt and pepper. Strain the sauce through a very fine sieve or several layers of cheesecloth. Just before serving, stir in the lemon juice.

This fast sauce can be used in place of the preceding sauce Allemande and is especially good with any poached fresh- or salt-water fish or with vegetables. Makes about 3 cups.

SAUCE VIN BLANC
(White-Wine Sauce)

> 2 cups fish stock*
> 2 tablespoons chopped shallots or green
>   onion bulbs
> 1 tablespoon finely chopped parsley
> Salt
> Freshly ground white pepper
> ½ cup dry white wine
> 6 tablespoons butter
> 4 tablespoons flour
> 1 cup heavy cream
> ∽ 3 egg yolks
> 1 tablespoon Cognac

Combine the fish stock, shallots, parsley, salt and pepper to taste, and the wine in a saucepan. Place over high heat and boil down or reduce by about one third. This will leave you with two thirds of the original liquid.

Melt 4 tablespoons of the butter, stir in the flour, and cook the *roux blanc* for a minute or two. Stir into the sauce and cook, stirring occasionally, for 10 to 15 minutes.

Whip the cream and yolks together, then combine the *liaison* (see Glossary) with the sauce, whipping vigorously with a wire whip. Strain through a fine sieve or several layers of cheesecloth. Stir in the remaining butter and the Cognac. Makes about 3 cups. Serve with poached fillets of sole, stuffed bass or porgy.

---

*Clam juice is a good substitute for homemade fish stock. If you use it, however, do not add salt until you taste for seasoning. Clam juice is available in 8-ounce bottles which is 1 cup.

CLASSIC HOLLANDAISE SAUCE

> ~ 4 egg yolks
>   2 tablespoons water
>   1½ cups clarified sweet butter (see Glossary),
>   about ¾ pound
>   Salt
>   Freshly ground white pepper
>   Cayenne
>   ½ tablespoon lemon juice (optional)

Place the egg yolks and water in the top of a double boiler (not aluminum). Beat for 1 minute with a whip, then place over medium heat or simmering water. Whip vigorously with a wire whip for 8 to 10 minutes, or until mixture is thick and creamy. Watch carefully to see that you do not curdle the eggs (should that happen, see page 88). The temperature should never be so hot you cannot dip your finger into the mixture. When perfectly combined, you can see the bottom of the pan between strokes and the sauce will be slow to cover the lines made by the whip.

Take off the heat, place pan on a damp cloth (this keeps the pan from turning as you beat), and add the hot butter very slowly, in dribbles, whipping constantly. Season with salt, pepper and cayenne to taste. (The salt will tend to thicken the Hollandaise slightly.) Stir in lemon juice last of all.

Keep warm in a pan of tepid water, not hot or your sauce will separate. (Hollandaise is always served lukewarm or tepid.) Makes 2 cups.

If it should be necessary to keep the sauce for any length of time before using, add 1 teaspoon of arrowroot to the yolks when beating them, or 2 tablespoons sauce Béchamel (see Glossary) to the finished sauce. This is known in the professional kitchen as bastardized Hollandaise.

BLENDER HOLLANDAISE

> ¾ pound sweet butter
> ∽ 4 egg yolks
> 2 tablespoons water
> Dash of salt
> Dash of freshly ground white pepper
> Dash of cayenne
> ½ tablespoon lemon juice

Melt the butter in a small saucepan over low heat until bubbling but not brown.

Place all the remaining ingredients in the container of an electric blender. Cover and turn motor to high. Immediately remove cover and quickly add the hot butter in a steady stream. When all the butter has been added, turn off the motor. Makes 1¾ cups.

Good as blender Hollandaise is, it does not match the classic recipe.

To salvage Hollandaise (either blender or classic) that has not thickened or has curdled: Place 1 teaspoon of lemon juice and 1 tablespoon of the sauce in a bowl that has been rinsed in hot water and dried. Beat with a wire whip until the sauce becomes creamy and thickens. Then whip in the remainder of the sauce, about 1 tablespoon at a time, whipping vigorously until it is creamy before adding the next tablespoon.

Leftover Hollandaise can be refrigerated successfully for a few days, or it can be frozen. To heat, place in a pan of tepid water until the right temperature has been reached; to thaw, bring out of the freezer a couple of hours before using; then heat as directed.

SAUCE MALTAISE

To 2 cups sauce Hollandaise, add the grated rind and strained juice of 1 navel orange. Usually served with asparagus or broccoli.

SAUCE MOUSSELINE

Sauce mousseline is a combination of 2 parts Hollandaise to 1 part heavy cream, whipped. To serve, place the whipped cream on top of the Hollandaise and allow the guests to help themselves, plunging through the cream into the sauce, which automatically mixes the two. Folded together in advance, the sauce would thin out.

BOILED DRESSING I

Boiled dressing is excellent with cold salmon, or to make salads such as potato or chicken. If it's too thick, it can always be diluted to the right consistency by adding heavy cream, oil or French dressing.

> ¼ teaspoon salt
> 1 teaspoon dry mustard
> 1½ tablespoons sugar
> Dash of cayenne
> 2 tablespoons flour
> 2 egg yolks, slightly beaten
> 1½ tablespoons melted butter
> ¾ cup milk
> ¼ cup vinegar

Mix all the dry ingredients together in the top of a double boiler. Stir in the egg yolks, butter, milk and vinegar. Cook over simmering water (take care that bottom of the pan is not *in* the water), stirring constantly, until the mixture has thickened. Strain through a fine sieve or several layers of cheesecloth. Cool. Makes about 1½ cups.

BOILED DRESSING II

> 2 tablespoons flour
> 1 teaspoon dry mustard
> 3 tablespoons sugar
> 1 cup dry white wine
> ½ cup wine vinegar or lemon juice
> ½ cup olive oil
> Salt
> Pepper
> ∽ 2 egg yolks, well beaten
> ¼ cup sour cream

Combine the flour, mustard, sugar, wine, and vinegar or lemon juice in the top of a double boiler. Add the oil and salt and pepper to taste to the well-beaten yolks. Stir into the flour mixture and cook over hot, not boiling, water, stirring constantly, until dressing has thickened. Take off the heat, cool slightly, then beat in the sour cream. Makes about 2 cups.

SAUCE CRÉMEUSE

> ∽ 3 egg yolks
> 6 tablespoons butter, softened
> ¼ teaspoon lemon juice
> Dash of salt
> Dash of white pepper

Place all the ingredients in a saucepan (not aluminum) over medium heat and whip very fast with a whip. Or place in the top of a double boiler and cook over simmering water, stirring constantly, for 3 or 4 minutes. Sauce crémeuse should be very light and fluffy. Makes 1 cup.

This is one of those good, useful French sauces to serve with vegetables or poached fish that can be made in 5 minutes just before serving.

AVGOLEMONO SAUCE

> 3 egg yolks
> 1 teaspoon arrowroot
> Salt
> Freshly ground white pepper
> 1 cup chicken broth
> 1 tablespoon finely chopped parsley
> 1 teaspoon lemon juice

Combine the egg yolks, arrowroot, and salt and pepper to taste in the top of a double boiler. Beat together with a wire whip, then add the chicken broth slowly, whipping constantly with the whip. Cook over moderate heat, whipping all the time, until sauce begins to thicken. Do not allow it to boil. When sauce has thickened sufficiently, it should coat the whip. Place over hot water to keep warm. Just before serving, stir in the parsley and lemon juice. Makes about 1 cup.

An excellent sauce to serve with roast leg of lamb.

SAUCE BÉARNAISE

½ cup wine or tarragon vinegar
1½ tablespoons chopped shallots
½ teaspoon freshly ground pepper
∿ 4 egg yolks, slightly beaten
1½ cups hot clarified sweet butter (see
   Glossary), about ¾ pound
Salt
1 teaspoon chopped fresh tarragon
1 teaspoon chopped parsley
½ teaspoon chopped fresh chervil (if
   available)

Combine the vinegar, shallots and pepper in a saucepan (not aluminum), and reduce over high heat until you have about ¼ cup left. This takes about 5 minutes. Cool slightly. Then gradually and briskly whip in the egg yolks with a wire whip. Place over very low heat and cook, whipping constantly, for 6 to 8 minutes. You should have a creamy sauce with the consistency of a soft whipped cream.

Take off the heat and add the hot butter, drop by drop, whipping steadily. Stir in the salt, strain the sauce, and add the chopped herbs.

Like Hollandaise, sauce Béarnaise is served lukewarm. It, too, is kept warm over tepid water. Makes about 2 cups.

Delicious with filet mignon, fried or boiled fish.

∿ NOTE: If you are apprehensive about cooking the sauce over direct heat, as instructed, pour reduced liquid into the top of a double boiler. When it has cooled, stir in the beaten egg yolks, place over simmering water, and cook to a creamy consistency, whipping constantly. This takes somewhat longer but it's undoubtedly safer.

CLASSIC MAYONNAISE

2 egg yolks
1 teaspoon French Dijon mustard
1 tablespoon tarragon or wine vinegar
Salt
Freshly ground white pepper
1½ cups imported peanut oil, vegetable oil,
  or olive oil*

Place the yolks, mustard, half of the vinegar, and salt and pepper to taste in a bowl. Beat for 1 minute with a wire whip. Add the oil slowly, drop by drop, whipping vigorously and constantly until all the oil is incorporated. If the finished mayonnaise seems too thick, beat in the remainder of the vinegar. Makes about 2 cups.

* Sometimes mayonnaise is made with half olive and half vegetable oil.

BLENDER MAYONNAISE

2 egg yolks
½ teaspoon dry mustard
½ teaspoon salt
2 tablespoons vinegar or lemon juice
1 cup vegetable oil, or half vegetable and
  half olive oil

Place the yolks, mustard, salt, vinegar and ¼ cup of the oil in the container of an electric blender. Cover container and turn motor to high. Immediately remove the cover and quickly add remaining oil in a steady stream. When all the oil is added, turn off the motor. Makes 1¼ cups.

To salvage curdled mayonnaise (either type): This happens to even the best cooks. Place 1 tablespoon of the curdled mayonnaise in a warm dry bowl with 1 teaspoon prepared French or domestic mustard. Whip with a wire whip until creamy. Add remaining mayonnaise, tablespoon by tablespoon, beating vigorously after each addition until creamy.

MAYONNAISE COLLÉE
(Gelatin Mayonnaise)

Combine 2 tablespoons white wine, 1 tablespoon wine vinegar, and 2½ tablespoons beef, chicken or fish stock in a small saucepan. Sprinkle 1 envelope unflavored gelatin over the liquid to soften. Then place over low heat and stir until the gelatin has dissolved. Cool to lukewarm.

Beat the lukewarm gelatin mixture gradually into 2 cups very thick mayonnaise. Taste for seasoning.

Mayonnaise collée should be used just before it sets, for coating cold dishes such as eggs, fish and vegetables, or molded salads.

ROQUEFORT CREAM MAYONNAISE

Whip ½ cup heavy cream until stiff. Crumble about 2 tablespoons Roquefort cheese. Fold the cream into 1 cup thick mayonnaise, then fold in the cheese.

Serve with green salads or hearts of lettuce.

SAUCE ANDALOUSE

Combine ½ cup very thick tomato purée with 2 cups very thick mayonnaise. Then fold in 1 sweet red pepper, seeded and finely chopped, and 1 teaspoon or so of chopped fresh tarragon or chives, or a mixture of the two.

Serve with cold chicken or hard-cooked eggs.

SAUCE GRIBICHE

1 hard-cooked egg, chopped
1 tablespoon chopped gherkins or small
  French sour pickles
1 tablespoon chopped drained capers
1 tablespoon chopped shallots or green
  onion bulbs
⅓ tablespoon chopped parsley
⅓ tablespoon chopped fresh tarragon
⅓ tablespoon chopped chives
Salt
Freshly ground white pepper
2 cups mayonnaise (page 93), for which
  you need 2 egg yolks

Mix all the ingredients together with a wooden spoon or spatula. If the sauce seems too thick, add just enough tepid water to bring it to the right consistency. Makes about 3 cups.

Sauce gribiche is especially good with all sorts of fried fish, or mixed with cold mussels when served as a first course.

SAUCE RÉMOULADE

To 1½ cups mayonnaise, add 1 generous teaspoon Dijon mustard, 2 tablespoons each of chopped gherkins, capers, parsley, fresh tarragon or chervil, and a "whisper" of anchovy paste. Allow the sauce to stand for a couple of hours to mellow.

Serve with sliced hard-cooked eggs, shellfish or cold meats.

SAUCE SUÉDOISE

To 1 cup thick mayonnaise, add ½ cup sweetened applesauce and a little freshly grated horseradish. Serve with cold pork or goose.

SAUCE TARTARE

To 1 cup mayonnaise, add 1 tablespoon each of finely chopped parsley, chives, fresh tarragon, fresh chervil (if available), well-drained capers, and 1 small sour pickle, finely chopped.

Serve with sautéed scallops, or poached or fried fish.

SAUCE VERTE
(Green Sauce)

2 tablespoons chopped watercress
2 tablespoons chopped spinach
1 tablespoon chopped parsley
½ tablespoon chopped fresh tarragon
1 tablespoon chopped chervil
1 tablespoon chopped chives
2 cups mayonnaise (page 93), for which
∽   you need 2 egg yolks

To make the classic sauce verte, the herbs should be used in the above proportions to 2 cups mayonnaise. If all the herbs are not available, omit those that are not and increase the others in proportion.

Blanch the herbs for 1 minute in boiling water, then refresh in cold water and drain thoroughly. Chop into a fine purée. Stir into the mayonnaise. Makes about 2½ cups.

Sauce verte is served with poached fish, such as salmon or trout.

∽ NOTE: The mayonnaise should be very thick because the juices of the herbs will thin it a little.

SAUCE *AÏOLI*

> 1 Idaho potato or California "long white,"
> baked or boiled in its skin
> 3 egg yolks
> 4 garlic cloves, chopped very fine
> Salt
> Good pinch of freshly ground white pepper
> Juice of ½ lemon
> 1½ cups salad oil

Scrape the pulp from the baked potato, or peel if boiled, and put through a ricer or food mill. Beat until very smooth. Then beat in the egg yolks and garlic, followed by salt to taste, the pepper and lemon juice, beating until thoroughly combined and absolutely smooth. This can best be done with an electric beater or in any electric mixer.

Now begin to add the oil slowly, drop by drop, beating constantly with wood *pilon* or spatula. When all the oil is in, the sauce should have the consistency of a firm mayonnaise, but watch carefully as you add the oil because if the sauce becomes too thick and sort of granular, it may separate. You can avoid this by adding a little lukewarm milk or water as you go along. Keep the finished sauce warm over warm water. Makes 3 to 4 cups.

Sauce Aïoli is served tepid with fish and especially salt-water fish.

COLD SAUCE AMÉRICAINE

Coral and creamy liver (tomalley) of
  poached hen lobsters
∽ 2 egg yolks
  1 tablespoon Dijon mustard
  1 tablespoon wine or tarragon vinegar
  ½ tablespoon paprika
  Salt
  Freshly ground white pepper
  1 cup vegetable oil

Chop the coral and mix with the liver (tomalley) to make a purée. To this add the egg yolks, mustard, vinegar, paprika, and salt and pepper to taste. Beat together with a whip for 1 minute. Begin to add the oil slowly, drop by drop, beating constantly until all the oil is incorporated. Makes about 2 cups.

Sauce Américaine is served with cold lobster and, customarily, with a julienne of Boston lettuce under sliced fresh ripe tomatoes.

RICH VINAIGRETTE

∽ 1 egg yolk
  2 tablespoons wine or tarragon vinegar
  1 tablespoon Dijon mustard
  1 tablespoon chopped shallots or green
    onion bulbs
  Salt
  Freshly ground white pepper
  ¾ cup salad oil

Combine the egg yolk, vinegar, mustard, shallots, and salt and pepper to taste. Whip together for about 1 minute. Add the oil very slowly, drop by drop, beating constantly with a wire whip. Makes 1 cup.

Serve with any kind of green salad.

BEURRE MONTPELLIER
(Green Butter)

~   3 egg yolks, in all
1 tablespoon chopped watercress
1 tablespoon chopped chives
1 tablespoon chopped parsley
1 tablespoon chopped shallots or green
onion bulbs
1 tablespoon chopped sour pickles
1 tablespoon chopped drained capers
1 tablespoon chopped anchovies
½ garlic clove, chopped
Salt
Pepper
Cayenne
½ pound butter, softened

Place 2 of the egg yolks in a cup or ramekin and cook in a small pan of simmering water, covered, for 15 to 20 minutes, until hard.

Blanch (see Glossary) the watercress, chives and parsley for 1 minute. Refresh in cold water, dry thoroughly, and chop fine along with shallots, pickles, capers, anchovies, garlic and the hard-cooked egg yolks. Add the remaining raw egg yolks and salt, pepper and cayenne to taste. Beat with a whip into a smooth purée. Beat in the softened butter, bit by bit, with a wooden spatula until thoroughly combined. Makes about 2 cups.

Buerre Montpellier is served with boiled or fried fish, steak or broiled meat. If with steak or broiled meat, it is customary to serve it sliced. Shape the butter into a roll, wrap in foil, Saran or wax paper, and refrigerate. Slice as needed.

Extra Yolks in ⌒ ⌒ ⌒
Desserts

FRESH PEACH KUCHEN

                2 cups sifted all-purpose flour
                ¼ teaspoon baking powder
                Dash of salt
                1 cup sugar
                ¼ pound butter
                6 fresh peaches, peeled and sliced
                1 teaspoon ground cinnamon
            ⌒   2 egg yolks
                1 cup sour cream

Sift the flour, baking powder, salt and 2 tablespoons of the sugar together. Work in the butter with the tips of your fingers or a pastry blender until the mixture looks mealy.

Lift the dough into an ungreased 8-inch-square pan and pat an even layer over the bottom and halfway up the sides. Arrange the peach slices on top of the pastry, overlapping slightly. Sprinkle the cinnamon mixed with the remaining sugar over the fruit and bake in a preheated 400° F. oven for 15 minutes.

Beat the yolks into the sour cream, pour over the Kuchen, and return the pan to the oven for 30 minutes longer. Serve warm.

GALETTE AU CITRON
(Lemon Pastry)

2 cups all-purpose flour
Dash of salt
Dash of sugar
½ cup plus 1 tablespoon lard or vegetable
   shortening, softened
½ cup water at room temperature

Filling

~ 4 egg yolks
1 cup sugar
2 tablespoons butter
Grated rind of 1 lemon
Strained juice of 1 lemon

Combine the flour, salt and sugar in a bowl and make a *fontaine* (a little hole) in the middle. Add the lard or vegetable shortening and water to the *fontaine*, and mix very fast with your fingers or a wooden spatula. When thoroughly mixed, refrigerate for about 20 minutes.

To make the filling, place all the ingredients in a bowl and beat together with a whip or electric beater for 5 minutes, whipping constantly.

To complete the *galette*, spread the chilled dough directly on a baking sheet, about ⅛ inch thick, shaping it like a pizza into a large round about 12 inches in diameter and as close to a circle as you can come. Now, make a wall all around the circle, about ½ inch high, by turning up the edge of the dough. Spoon the lemon mixture over the circle, smoothing it with a spatula, and bake in a preheated 400° F. oven for 25 to 30 minutes, or until crust is nicely browned. If it starts to get too brown on top to be attractive, protect it with a piece of foil. Serves 6.

GÂTEAU SUISSE

1 large (1 pound) potato
5 squares (1-ounce size) unsweetened
  chocolate
⅜ pound (1½ sticks) butter
1½ cups sugar
1 teaspoon vanilla extract
1 teaspoon powdered instant coffee
2 egg yolks

Boil the potato in its jacket until tender when tested with a small pointed knife. Butter very generously an oblong 1-quart metal loaf pan (metal because it is so much easier to release the cake than from earthenware). Melt chocolate over hot, not boiling, water.

Work butter with your hands or with an electric beater until creamy. Then beat in the sugar gradually. Add vanilla, instant coffee and egg yolks. Beat very hard at high speed with an electric beater. Stir in the chocolate. Mash the hot potato thoroughly through a sieve, food mill or potato ricer. Add to the chocolate mixture. Beat again with the electric beater until smooth. Spoon into prepared mold and refrigerate, covered, until firm; at least 3 hours.

To serve, carefully run a knife around the edge of the pan, right to the bottom. Then place bottom of pan in hot water until it loosens. Turn out onto a serving platter and score the top with the tines of a fork. Refrigerate again until firm. This extraordinarily rich cake (it's closer to fudge than cake) should be served in very thin slices and, as you will discover, needs no further adornment.

RICE IMPÉRATRICE

> 1 cup mixed candied fruits, diced
> ¼ cup kirsch or Cognac
> 1 quart milk
> ½ cup uncooked long-grain rice
> 1½ cups granulated sugar
> ∾ 4 egg yolks
> 1 tablespoon vanilla extract
> ½ teaspoon salt
> 1 teaspoon grated lemon rind
> 3 envelopes unflavored gelatin
> 2 cups heavy cream
> ½ cup sifted confectioners' sugar

Sauce

> 1 pint raspberries or strawberries
> 1 cup granulated sugar

Combine the candied fruits with the kirsch or Cognac in a bowl. Set aside and keep at room temperature.

Scald the milk in the top of a double boiler, add the rice, and stir until all the grains are well separated. Cook, covered, for 50 to 55 minutes, giving the mixture an occasional stir. Combine the granulated sugar, yolks, vanilla, salt, lemon rind and gelatin. Stir into the rice and cook for about 5 minutes, stirring constantly. Take off the heat, pour into a clean bowl, and refrigerate. Stir occasionally.

When the mixture is cold and begins to set, add the candied fruits (reserve half the liqueur to use in the sauce). Then fold in the cream, whipped and blended with the confectioners' sugar. Pour into a 1½- to 2-quart mold and refrigerate.

To make the sauce, blend the raspberries or hulled strawberries with the sugar in an electric blender at high speed for 30 seconds. Place in a saucepan, bring to a rolling boil, then simmer for a couple of minutes. Strain through a fine sieve or several layers of cheesecloth. Refrigerate. When cold, stir in the liqueur reserved from the candied fruit.

To serve, unmold the rice on a chilled serving platter and spoon some of the cold sauce over the top. Pour the remainder of the sauce into a cold serving dish. Serves 6 to 8.

CHOCOLATE AND RUM EGGNOG IN A PASTRY SHELL

> 1 envelope unflavored gelatin
> ½ cup cold water
> 2 squares (1-ounce size) unsweetened chocolate
> 3 egg yolks
> ¾ cup sugar
> 2 tablespoons dark rum
> 1 cup heavy cream
> 1 baked 8-inch pie shell

Sprinkle the gelatin over the water in a saucepan to soften. Add the chocolate. Place directly over low heat and stir constantly until mixture is well blended and the gelatin has dissolved.

Beat the yolks until very thick, then beat in the sugar gradually. Stir in the chocolate mixture and rum. Cool.

Beat the cream until thick, then gently fold in the chocolate mixture with a spatula. Chill in refrigerator until mixture just begins to take a shape. Spoon into the baked pie shell and refrigerate, covered, for several hours, or until firm.

To serve, garnish with rosettes of whipped cream around the perimeter of the pie. Serves 6.

SABAYON AU VIN BLANC
(White-Wine Sabayon)

∽ 4 egg yolks
1 cup sugar
1 cup dry white wine or dry sherry or dry vermouth

Combine the yolks and sugar in a bowl (not aluminum) or in the top of a double boiler. Beat with an electric beater for 2 minutes. Slowly add the wine, then place over hot, not boiling, water and cook, whipping constantly with a wire whip, for 8 to 10 minutes. You should have a creamy fluffy mixture with enough body to leave a clear path when you pull the whip through it. At the end of the cooking time, pour sabayon into a clean bowl and chill in the refrigerator. Serves 4.

∽ NOTE: If made with dry sherry or dry vermouth, the sabayon takes on an ivory color. However, the flavor is as delicious as when made with white wine.

CRÈME BRÛLÉE

2 cups light cream
∽ 4 egg yolks
2½ tablespoons granulated sugar
Pinch of salt
1 teaspoon vanilla extract
2 tablespoons firmly packed sifted brown sugar

Heat the cream until a film shines on the top, but do not allow it to boil. Beat the yolks until they are pale and thick. Gradually beat in the granulated sugar and the salt. Add the hot cream very slowly, stirring constantly. Flavor with the vanilla. Pour into a 1-quart baking dish.

Set the dish in a pan of hot water, which should reach to about two thirds of the depth of the baking dish. Bake in a preheated 350° F. oven for 1 hour, or until a knife plunged into the center comes out dry. Refrigerate until cold.

When cold, sift the brown sugar evenly over the surface. Broil 4 to 5 inches from broiling unit until the sugar melts and forms a hard surface. This takes only a minute or two, so don't even shut the oven door. Chill in the refrigerator until cold before serving. Serves 4.

PETITS POTS DE CRÈME VANILLE
(Rich Vanilla Custard)

> 1¼ cups sugar
> 10 egg yolks
> ¼ teaspoon arrowroot
> 1½ tablespoons vanilla extract
> 1 quart milk

Combine the sugar, yolks, arrowroot and vanilla in a generous bowl and whip together with a wire whip for about 5 minutes, or until the mixture becomes pale yellow and "makes ribbons" (page 39). Bring the milk to a boil, then add to the yolk mixture very gradually in a thin stream, whipping constantly. Strain through a fine sieve or several layers of cheesecloth. Allow to stand for 2 or 3 minutes, then remove any foam that rises to the top.

Pour into 6 or 8 individual molds or ramekins or *petits pots*. Set them in a large baking pan, add enough hot water to reach to about half the depth of the molds, and bake in a preheated 400° F. oven for 30 minutes. Do not allow the water in the pan to boil or custard will become grainy. Should it boil, add enough cold water to stop the boiling.

Pots de crème are served right in their little pots and never unmolded. They should be ice cold. Serve with *petits fours secs* (see Glossary).

MOUSSE AU CHOCOLAT

∽ 4 egg yolks
¾ cup sugar
1 teaspoon powdered instant coffee or
⅓ cup strong coffee concentrate
6 tablespoons butter, softened
8 squares (1-ounce size) sweet cooking
chocolate*
⅓ cup milk
2 tablespoons Grand Marnier or
grated rind of ½ orange (optional)
2 cups heavy cream

Combine the yolks, sugar, and coffee in the top of a double boiler. Place over simmering water and cook, beating constantly with a wire whip, for 5 minutes. The mixture should double in volume and have a creamy consistency. Take off the heat, place in a pan of cold water, and beat hard with a whip for 2 to 3 minutes, or until mixture reaches room temperature. The cream will thicken and get quite pasty. Beat in the softened butter (which should also be at room temperature), a small amount at a time, until well mixed.

Meanwhile, combine the chocolate and milk in a saucepan. Stir over moderate heat until chocolate has melted and you have a very smooth shiny mixture. Combine with the egg mixture, stirring until well mixed. Add the liqueur or orange rind.

Whip the cream until thick but not butter. Add about one fourth to the chocolate cream, beating it in with a wire whip. Fold in the remaining cream with a spatula. Pour the mousse into a serving dish and refrigerate for at least 2 to 3 hours. Serve with whipped cream or plain. Serves 10.

Mousse au chocolat makes a splendid party dessert because it can be made a day or two ahead, if you wish.

*One ounce of any sweet cooking chocolate is the equivalent of 1 ounce of semisweet chocolate pieces or 1 square (1-ounce size) of semisweet chocolate.

Grand Marnier or orange rind are often added to chocolate cream or mousse because the orange flavor blends so perfectly with chocolate. If you wish to perfume your mousse au chocolat with either one, combine with the chocolate mixture before adding the whipped cream.

BAVAROIS AU CAFÉ
(Coffee Bavarian Cream)

> 1 cup granulated sugar
> 8 egg yolks
> 3 envelopes unflavored gelatin
> ¼ cup concentrated liquid coffee or
>   3 tablespoons powdered instant coffee*
> 2½ cups milk
> 2 cups heavy cream
> ¼ cup sifted confectioners' sugar

Combine the granulated sugar, yolks, gelatin and coffee in a large bowl. Bring the milk to a boil in the top of a double boiler. Add it very gradually to the yolk mixture, in a thin stream, whipping vigorously with a wire whip. Pour back into the top of the double boiler and place it over simmering water. Cook, stirring constantly with a wooden spatula, until mixture has thickened, or reaches 180° F. on a thermometer. Do not allow it to boil.

Strain through a very fine sieve or several layers of cheesecloth into a clean bowl. Cover surface with Saran so a skin doesn't form on top. Refrigerate.

When the mixture just begins to set, whip the cream until almost stiff, then gradually add the confectioners' sugar, beating constantly. Take care not to overbeat or cream will turn to butter. Fold the cream into the *Bavarois* with a spatula. Pour into a mold (1½ to 2 quarts) and refrigerate until firm.

* Preferably made with espresso coffee.

To unmold, carefully run a knife around the edge of mold and invert on serving platter. If mold does not release immediately, wrap top in a hot cloth for a few seconds.

Serve with Crème Anglaise (English Cream, below). Serves 6 to 8.

CRÈME ANGLAISE
(English Cream)

∽ 8 egg yolks
1 cup sugar
1 tablespoon vanilla extract
1 tablespoon arrowroot
2½ cups milk

Combine the yolks, sugar, vanilla and arrowroot in a bowl and beat with a wire whip or electric beater, or in the electric mixer, until the mixture "makes ribbons" (page 39), 5 to 6 minutes. Properly beaten, it will be pale yellow and heavy.

Bring the milk to a boil and add to egg mixture in a slow steady stream, whipping constantly. Pour into the top of a double boiler and cook over simmering water, stirring constantly with a wooden spatula, until cream has thickened and will coat a spoon, or reaches about 175° F. on a thermometer.

Strain through a fine sieve or several layers of cheesecloth and chill. Makes about 4 cups.

ORANGE CUSTARD SAUCE

Beat together 3 egg yolks, ¼ cup sugar and 2 tablespoons cornstarch until very thick and creamy. Pour into the top of a double boiler and stir in the grated rind and strained juice of 1 good, big orange. Cook, over hot water, stirring constantly, until the mixture has thickened. Then stir in the strained juice of ½ a lemon. Cool. When cool, fold in ½ cup heavy cream, whipped. Chill.

SOUFFLÉ GLACÉ GRAND MARNIER

> 1¾ cups sifted confectioners' sugar
> 8 egg yolks
> ½ cup Grand Marnier
> 3 cups heavy cream
> Powdered cocoa (optional)

First, make a collar (page 203) for a 1½-quart soufflé dish and set aside.

Combine the sugar and egg yolks in a large bowl and beat with an electric beater, or preferably in an electric mixer, for 25 to 30 minutes. At this point the mixture should have a pastelike appearance and be very thick and creamy. Begin to add the Grand Marnier very slowly in a steady stream, beating constantly. When all the liqueur has been incorporated, beat for 5 minutes longer.

Whip the cream with a rotary or electric beater until it begins to take shape. Add to the egg mixture and beat together for 3 to 4 minutes. If the mixture seems firm, spoon into the prepared mold at once. If it seems too soft, place bowl in the freezing compartment of the refrigerator. Once it has begun to set, pour carefully into the mold right up to the rim. Add the collar (page 203) and the remainder of the mixture. Place in the freezing compartment of the refrigerator for 3 to 4 hours.

About 5 minutes before serving time, remove the soufflé from the freezer and place in refrigerator. At serving time, pull the paper collar away from the soufflé with the greatest care and, if you wish, sprinkle the top with a little powdered cocoa to make it look hot and delicately browned.

Cold soufflés are served directly from the soufflé dish. Serves 8.

ANGEL'S PAPER

>   Butter
> ∞   6 egg yolks
>   1 cup sugar
>   Juice of 2 oranges
>   Juice of 1 lemon

Butter 6 custard cups well. Beat the egg yolks vigorously until very thick and creamy. Divide the beaten yolks among the little cups evenly. Place in the center of a preheated 375° F. oven and bake for 10 minutes.

Meanwhile, combine sugar and orange and lemon juices in a heavy saucepan at least 8 inches in diameter. Stir until the sugar has dissolved and the mixture comes to a boil. Allow it to simmer while the egg yolks cook.

Turn the cooked yolks into the bubbling syrup, bring the heat up to moderate, and cook 2 minutes, basting with the syrup.

Refrigerate overnight. Serve cold, one to each person, with a spoonful of the syrup.

BISCUIT TORTONI

>   ⅔ cup milk
>   ½ cup sugar
> ∞   6 egg yolks
>   1 cup finely crushed crisp macaroons
>   ½ cup chopped almonds, toasted lightly
>   ½ cup heavy cream
>   1 teaspoon vanilla extract
>   2 tablespoons sherry

Pour the milk into the top of a double boiler and heat over direct heat until it comes to a boil and a film shines on the surface; in other words, scald. Add the sugar and stir until dissolved.

Beat the egg yolks slightly, stir a little of the hot milk into the yolks, and pour back into top of the double boiler. Cook over hot, not boiling, water for 5 minutes, stirring occasionally. Cool.

When cold, mix in the crushed macaroons and half of the almonds. Whip the cream until stiff, then mix in the vanilla and sherry. Fold into the yolk mixture gently with a spatula and pour into a refrigerator tray. Sprinkle remaining almonds over the top and freeze until firm.

About 30 minutes before serving, remove the tray from the freezing compartment to refrigerator. To serve, spoon Tortoni into individual serving dishes. Serves 8.

GELATO DI ALBICOCCHE
(*Apricot Ice Cream*)

> 2 cups heavy cream
> 8 egg yolks
> 2 very thin slices of lemon rind
> ¼ cup sugar (about)
> 1 jar (12 ounces) apricot preserves

Mix the cream with the yolks in the top of a double boiler. Add the lemon rind and cook over simmering water, stirring constantly with a wire whip, until mixture has thickened or coats a spoon. When the custard reaches the right consistency, stir in the sugar, or a little more, to taste. As you do this, remember, the apricot preserves are sweetened. Remove lemon rind and cool the custard.

Meanwhile, place the jar of apricot preserves in a small saucepan of warm water, over low heat, until the preserves have melted, but are not hot. Stir occasionally. Actually, this takes only a few minutes. Then push through a sieve to make a smooth purée.

When the custard is cold, stir in the apricot purée very thoroughly. Pour the mixture into ice-cube trays and place in the freezer for about 4 hours, or until firm. Give the mixture a stir when you think of it. Serves 8.

NOTE: This does not turn into a hard ice cream, but has a rather soft creamy consistency.

GLACE AUX AMANDES
(Almond Ice Cream)

∽ 8 egg yolks
1½ cups sugar
1 can (8-ounce size) commercial almond paste
less 2 tablespoons*
2 cups milk
1 cup heavy cream

Combine the egg yolks, sugar and almond paste, crumbled. Work together with an electric beater or in an electric mixer until mixture is pale yellow and everything is homogeneous.

Bring the milk to a boil in the top of a double boiler, then add it to the egg mixture in a slow steady stream, mixing vigorously. Pour back into the top of the double boiler and cook over simmering water, stirring constantly with a wooden spatula, until mixture has thickened or reached 165° F. to 170° F. on a thermometer.

Take off the heat, stir in the cream, then strain through a fine sieve or several layers of cheesecloth. Refrigerate until cool, stirring occasionally. When cold, pour into the container of an electric freezer. Pack the freezer with layers of cracked ice and coarse salt until full. Freeze according to manufacturer's instructions until ice cream is firm, about 20 minutes. When the motor sounds "tired," it will have frozen sufficiently.

Spoon into a 1-quart mold, cover the mold, and place in the freezer, or in the freezing compartment of the refrigerator. Lacking either a freezer or large enough freezing compartment, pack the securely covered mold in layers of ice and rock salt to freeze until hard.

Serve *en coupe,* in other words, spooned into a serving dish. Serves 8.

* Or grind ¾ cup blanched almonds in an electric blender until fine, then mix with 6 tablespoons granulated sugar. This can be used instead of the commercial almond paste.

PART III

Extra Whites in ∽ ∽ ∽

Cocktail Fare
Entrées
Little Cakes
Desserts
Frostings

Extra Whites in ~ ~ ~
Cocktail Fare

FROZEN CHEESE

½ pound Roquefort, blue or Cheddar cheese
∾ 2 egg whites, stiffly beaten
Dash of Tabasco
¾ cup heavy cream, whipped

Work the cheese until soft and pliable, then combine thoroughly with stiffly beaten whites. Add Tabasco to taste and the whipped cream. Spoon into a 3-cup mold and freeze.

To serve, unmold on a bed of crushed ice and serve with piping hot unflavored crackers. Serves 8 to 10.

PETS DE NONNE AU FROMAGE
(Cheese Fritters)

∾ 2 egg whites
Dash of salt
¾ cup grated Swiss cheese
2 slices of bread, crumbled into fine crumbs
Vegetable oil for deep frying

Beat the egg whites with the salt in an electric mixer or with an electric beater until they stand in peaks when you hold up the beater. Add the cheese and beat at low speed for 1 minute. Fold in bread crumbs (bread can be "crumbed" in the electric blender). Form the mixture into little balls about the size of marbles.

Heat the oil in a deep fryer to 350° F. on a thermometer. Drop the little balls into the oil (don't crowd the pan) and cook for about 2 minutes, or until golden brown. Lift out of oil with a slotted spoon and drain on paper towels.

Serve in a napkin-lined dish. Serves 6 to 8.

CROÛTES AU JAMBON
(Ham Soufflé on Toast)

Unsliced firm day-old bread
1 cup finely diced cooked ham
½ cup Sauce Béchamel*
⌒　2 egg whites
⅓ cup freshly grated Parmesan cheese

Cut off 9 or 10 bread slices ½ inch thick; trim off the crusts and cut slices into halves or quarters. Stir the ham into the hot Béchamel.

Beat the egg whites until they stand in peaks when you hold up the beater. Fold gently into the ham mixture with a rubber spatula. Spread the bread pieces with the ham mixture about 1 inch thick. Place on a baking sheet, sprinkle with the cheese, and bake in a preheated 425° F. oven for 12 to 15 minutes, or until golden brown. Serve at once. A delicious hors-d'oeuvre.

*Make the Sauce Béchamel (see Glossary) in these proportions: 1½ tablespoons butter, 1½ tablespoons flour, ½ cup milk, seasoned with a dash each of salt, freshly ground pepper and freshly grated nutmeg.

Extra Whites in ◡ ◡ ◡
Entrées

SHAD ROE MOUSSE WITH SORREL SAUCE

> 3 pairs small shad roe
> 3 cups heavy cream
> ◡ 3 egg whites
> Salt
> Freshly-ground pepper
> Paprika
> Sorrel Sauce (next page)

Butter a 9-inch ring mold (not aluminum) very thoroughly and refrigerate.

Cut the shad roes apart, and remove as much of the filmy skin as possible. Purée a small amount at a time in the electric blender, using the lowest speed. Place in a generous bowl with the cream and egg whites and seasonings to taste. Beat steadily with an electric beater or electric mixer for about 10 minutes.

Pour the mixture into the prepared mold and place in the refrigerator for 30 minutes or so.

To bake, place in a pan of boiling water, which should reach to two-thirds the depth of the mold. Bake in a preheated 350° F. oven for 1 hour and 15 minutes, or until a knife inserted in the center comes out dry.

To serve, unmold onto a warm serving platter. Spoon some

of the sorrel sauce over the ring and serve the remainder on the side. Serves 6.

Sorrel Sauce

1½ cups Sauce Béchamel*
½ cup heavy cream
Salt
White pepper
½ tablespoon butter
¼ cup, about, fresh sorrel cut in fine julienne
2 tablespoons capers, well drained

Bring the Béchamel up to simmer, then beat in the cream, a small amount at a time, until the sauce is lightly thickened. Taste for seasoning. Set aside for the moment.

Melt the butter. When foaming, add the shredded sorrel and simmer for 5 to 6 minutes. Strain off any surplus juice and stir the sorrel into the cream sauce. Bring to a simmer again, then add the capers.

* Make the Sauce Béchamel (see Glossary) in these proportions: 2 tablespoons butter, 1½ tablespoons flour, 1½ cups milk, and salt and white pepper to taste.

Classic French recipes calling for fish such as *Pain de Poisson, Mousse* and *Quenelles* are, as Jacques points out, "pretty tricky." "In the professional kitchen," he continues, "the fish is pounded or 'pestled' with a big wood rammer. It is then crushed, along with the egg whites, and afterwards pushed through a metal screen (sieve) with a wooden 'mushroom.' Done this way, the result is a very homogeneous and firm-textured *chair à poisson*

(fish flesh). Unfortunately, it is very 'involving' and more complicated than most housewives would want to cope with. For a small quantity of fish, the blender is an adequate substitute." Therefore, the recipes for both the *Pain de Poisson* and *Mousse de Sole* are given with the assumption that you are equipped with an electric blender.

PAIN DE POISSON
(Fish Loaf)

> ½ cup milk
> 3 slices of bread, crumbled
> 1 pound boned skinned fish (flounder, codfish, haddock)*
> 5 egg whites
> Salt
> Freshly ground white pepper
> 1 cup Sauce Béchamel**

Pour the milk into a bowl, add the crumbled bread, and set aside.

Cut the fish into small pieces. Place half of the fish and half of the whites with a dash each of salt and pepper in the container of an electric blender. Blend for about 1 minute, or until you have a smooth firm-textured paste. Transfer to a clean bowl. Blend remaining fish and remaining egg whites in exactly the same way. Combine with the first mixture and refrigerate.

Make the sauce Béchamel and place a piece of Saran right on top of the sauce to prevent a skin forming; cool in the refrigerator. When the sauce has cooled, combine it with the fish mixture thoroughly.

* Almost any kind of fish, even fresh-water fish, can be used, but avoid dry fish such as swordfish.
** Make the Sauce Béchamel (see Glossary) in these proportions: 3 tablespoons butter, 3 tablespoons flour, 1 cup milk. Season with salt and freshly ground white pepper.

Work the bread and milk mixture into a paste, then work it into the fish mixture. Add salt and pepper to taste. You'll notice it takes quite a lot of salt to bring up the flavor of the fish. Butter a mold (preferably a deep rectangular pâté mold) and spoon the fish mixture into it. Cover top with wax paper and bake in a preheated 425° F. oven for 50 to 60 minutes.

To serve, unmold, slice and arrange on a hot platter. Serve with Sauce Bercy (page 125) and *pommes à l'anglaise* (plain boiled potatoes). Serves 6 to 8.

MOUSSE DE SOLE

> 1 pound boned skinned fish (imported English sole or flounder fillets)
> ⌒ 5 egg whites
> 1¾ cups heavy cream, well chilled
> Salt
> Freshly ground pepper

Prepare the fish with the egg whites exactly as you do in Pain de Poisson (preceding recipe). Once you have combined the fish and egg whites into a homogeneous paste, place the bowl with the mixture on ice. Work vigorously with a wooden spoon or flat spatula, adding the cold heavy cream very slowly, almost drop by drop, as you add oil in making mayonnaise. This is rather ticklish and if the mixture even looks as if it might separate, add a little pinch of salt, which usually helps to tighten it.

When all the cream is in, and you have a smooth firm-textured mixture, season with salt and pepper to taste. Spoon into a buttered round 1½-quart mold, cover with wax paper, and set the mold in a pan of hot water (water should reach to about half the depth of the mold). Bake in a preheated 425° F. oven for 1 hour. When baked, take out of the oven and keep warm in a pan of hot water.

At serving time, unmold on a heated platter, spoon Sauce Bercy (below) over the mousse, and serve with small freshly boiled potatoes. Serves 8.

~ NOTE: If, by some horrible mischance, the mixture separates in the process of adding the cream, the whole business can be salvaged by turning the mousse into a Pain de Poisson (page 123). Stir into the remaining cream 2 tablespoons arrowroot or 3 tablespoons flour until smooth. Add 3 slices of bread crumbled fine, and mix until well combined. Spoon into a buttered mold and bake and serve as directed for Pain de Poisson.

SAUCE BERCY FOR FISH

2 cups fish broth*
2 tablespoons chopped shallots or
  green-onion bulbs
2 tablespoons finely chopped parsley, in all
Salt
Freshly ground white pepper
½ cup dry white wine
6 tablespoons butter, in all
4 tablespoons flour

* Bottled clam juice is a good substitute for homemade fish stock. If you use it, do not, however, add salt until you taste for seasoning.

Combine the fish broth, shallots, 1 tablespoon of the parsley, salt, pepper, and wine in a saucepan. Place over high heat and boil down, that is, reduce, by about one third. This will leave you two thirds of the original quantity.

Melt 4 tablespoons of the butter, stir in the flour, and cook this *roux blanc* for a minute or two. Stir the reduced broth into the *roux* and cook, stirring occasionally, for 10 to 15 minutes. Add the remaining butter and parsley. Makes about 3 cups.

Serve with Mousse de Sole or Pain de Poisson (see preceding recipes), or with poached fillet of sole, bass, or porgy.

SAUTÉED FISH FILLETS

> Fillets of flounder, porgy, or fresh cod
> (or shrimps or scallops)
> Flour
> ~ Egg-white coating (next page)
> Fresh bread crumbs
> Butter

Dip the fish fillets or shellfish into flour and gently shake off any excess. Then dip into the egg-white coating, finally into the crumbs. Be sure the pieces are entirely coated. Sauté the fish quickly in hot butter until golden on both sides. Lift carefully from the pan and drain on paper towels. Serve with lemon wedges or with tomato sauce (see Glossary).

Egg-white coating

2 egg whites
¼ cup salad oil
¼ cup water
Dash of salt
Dash of freshly ground white pepper

Combine all the ingredients in a bowl and beat together with a whip or rotary beater until you have a smooth mixture. Makes 1 cup. This will keep, refrigerated, for 2 or 3 days.

*M*OUSSE OF HAM

3 envelopes unflavored gelatin
2 cups Sauce Velouté*
1 pound ham,** diced
Salt
Freshly ground white pepper
3 egg whites
⅛ teaspoon cream of tartar
1 cup heavy cream, whipped

Stir the gelatin into the hot sauce velouté and cook for about 2 minutes, stirring constantly, until gelatin has dissolved.

Place half of the diced ham and half of the sauce in the container of an electric blender. Blend at high speed for 35 to 40 seconds. Empty mixture into a saucepan. Blend remaining ham and sauce. Combine the two and taste for seasoning, adding salt and pepper if necessary. Keep warm over medium heat.

* Make the Sauce Velouté (see Glossary) in these proportions: 3 tablespoons butter, 3 tablespoons flour, 2 cups chicken broth.
** Chicken, duck or liver, in the same amount, can be substituted for the ham.

Beat the whites with the cream of tartar until they stand in peaks when you hold up the beater. With a wooden spatula, fold at once into the hot ham mixture, carefully but thoroughly. (*Note:* The beaten egg whites are added to the hot ham mixture to cook them, unlike the whipped cream, which must be added when mixture is cold.) Refrigerate, giving mixture an occasional stir with spatula until almost cool and beginning to set.

Fold the whipped cream into the cooled mixture and spoon into a mold.* Refrigerate for at least 3 hours, or until firm. Serves 10.

* If the mold is lined with aspic, the ham mixture should be almost set before spooning into the mold. To line a mold, see Aspic in the Glossary.

FRICADELLES DE VEAU SMITANE
(Veal Patties with Sour Cream)

∽ 3 egg whites
1 pound lean veal, very finely ground
6 slices of firm day-old bread
¼ cup milk
Salt
Freshly ground white pepper
1⅔ cups heavy cream
4 tablespoons butter
2 tablespoons vegetable oil
½ small onion, chopped
3 tablespoons vinegar

Combine the egg whites and the meat in a bowl and beat with a wooden spatula vigorously. Work 3 slices of the bread together with all the milk into a smooth paste. Add to the meat mixture, combining the two well. Season to taste with salt and pepper. Beat in ⅔ cup of the cream slowly, beating hard and constantly with a spatula. When all the cream has been added you should have a firm but fluffy mixture.

Take remaining bread and crumble fine; this can be done by hand or in the electric blender; place crumbs in a bowl. Divide the meat mixture into 8 equal parts, roll in the crumbs, then flatten into rounds or disks. Heat 2 tablespoons of the butter and all the oil in a frying pan. When hot, sauté the veal "disks" slowly until golden brown on both sides. Allow 10 to 12 minutes all told.

To make the sauce, melt remaining butter in a frying pan, add the onion, and sauté until transparent and touched with gold. Add the vinegar, bring to a boil, then add the remaining cream and salt and pepper to taste. Reduce the heat and boil slowly for 2 or 3 minutes. Strain through a fine sieve or several layers of cheesecloth.

To serve, arrange the *fricadelles* on a hot serving platter, with sauce spooned over them. Serve with buttered tiny peas or sautéed string beans. Serves 8.

CHEESE SOUFFLÉ AUX BLANCS

6 egg whites
¼ teaspoon cream of tartar
1 cup Sauce Béchamel*
1¼ cups coarsely grated Swiss Cheese

* Make the Sauce Béchamel (see Glossary) in these proportions: 3 tablespoons butter, 3 tablespoons flour, 1 cup milk, seasoned with salt and freshly ground white pepper.

Prepare a 1-quart soufflé mold, coating it with finely grated cheese (page 203). Refrigerate.

Beat the whites with the cream of tartar until they stand in peaks when you lift up the beater. Add about one third of the beaten whites to the slightly cooled sauce Béchamel, whipping them in vigorously with a whip. Fold in the remaining whites and the cheese with a wooden or rubber spatula.

Pour into the prepared soufflé mold and bake in a preheated 400° F. oven for 25 to 30 minutes. If, during the baking, the top begins to brown too fast, cover with a piece of foil for the remainder of the cooking time. Serve immediately. Serves 6.

WELSH RAREBIT PLAZA ATHÉNÉE

1 cup Sauce Béchamel*
〜 4 egg whites
¼ teaspoon cream of tartar
½ teaspoon baking powder
1½ cups grated Swiss cheese
5 slices of white bread, toasted

Make the sauce Béchamel and set aside.

Beat the egg whites with the cream of tartar until they stand in peaks when you lift up the beater. Whip one third of the whites

* Make the Sauce Béchamel (see Glossary) in these proportions: 3 tablespoons butter, 3 tablespoons flour, 1 cup milk. Season with salt, freshly ground white pepper and freshly grated nutmeg.

and the baking powder into the sauce Béchamel vigorously with a wire whip. Then fold in half of the cheese and the remaining whites carefully with a wooden or rubber spatula.

Press the toasted bread into ramekins or custard cups, pushing it down to the bottom. Fill with the soufflé mixture and sprinkle some of the remaining cheese on top of each ramekin. Bake in a preheated 400° F. oven for 20 to 25 minutes. Serves 5.

This makes a delicious luncheon dish.

SOUFFLÉ À L'AUBERGINE
(*Eggplant Soufflé*)

> 1 large eggplant
> 1 cup vegetable oil
> 1 medium onion, coarsely chopped
> 2 garlic cloves, chopped
> Salt
> Freshly ground pepper
> 4 egg whites
> Dash of cream of tartar
> ½ cup freshly grated Parmesan cheese

Cut the eggplant lengthwise into halves and place them in a baking pan. Cover with ½ cup of the oil and cook in a preheated 400° F. oven for 25 minutes. Remove from oven and scrape out the pulp with a spoon, taking care not to break the skin. Chop the pulp coarsely. Chill the skin in the refrigerator.

Pour the remaining oil into a skillet, add the onion, and sauté for 2 or 3 minutes; add the chopped eggplant and garlic and salt and pepper to taste. Cook over medium heat for 6 to 8 minutes; take off the heat and cool to room temperature.

Whip the egg whites with the cream of tartar until they stand in peaks when you hold up the beater. Beat about one third of the whites into the eggplant mixture, whipping together well. Fold in the remaining whites with a spatula. Place the chilled skins on a baking sheet and fill each with half of the mixture. Sprinkle tops with the Parmesan. Place in a preheated 400° F. oven and bake for 25 minutes. Serve immediately. Serves 4.

SPINACH SOUFFLÉ

2 tablespoons butter
1 cup packed down coarsely chopped spinach*
Salt
Freshly ground pepper
Freshly grated nutmeg
1 garlic clove, minced
½ cup Sauce Béchamel**
∾ 5 egg whites
¼ teaspoon cream of tartar
Croutons (see Glossary)

Prepare a 1-quart soufflé mold, coating it with fine bread crumbs or grated cheese (page 203). Refrigerate.

Place the butter in a small saucepan and allow it to become foaming and almost black. This is important for flavor. Mix in the spinach with a wooden spatula, adding a dash each of salt, pepper and nutmeg, and the garlic. Cover and simmer over low heat for 5 minutes. Then stir in the sauce Béchamel until you have a homogeneous texture.

Beat the egg whites with the cream of tartar until stiff when

* If frozen spinach is used, thaw, press out as much of the water as possible, then chop coarsely.
** Make the Sauce Béchamel (see Glossary) in these proportions: 3 tablespoons butter, 3 tablespoons flour, ½ cup milk. Season with salt and freshly ground black pepper.

you hold up the beater. Whip one third of the whites into the spinach mixture, whipping them in thoroughly. Fold in the remaining whites and the croutons carefully with a spatula. Pour into the prepared soufflé mold and bake in a preheated 400° F. oven for 25 to 30 minutes. Serves 6.

OTHER USES FOR EGG WHITES

One of the very best ways to use extra egg whites is for clarifying aspic or consommé. Recipes for these procedures are in Part IV on pages 170 and 171.

Extra Whites in ~ ~ ~
Little Cakes

DÉLICES AU CHOCOLAT

> ¼ pound butter
> ½ cup sugar
> Dash of vanilla extract
> 2 egg whites
> ⅓ cup all-purpose flour
> 8 squares (1-ounce size) semisweet chocolate or
>   1½ packages (6-ounce size) semisweet choc-
>   olate pieces

Grease a baking sheet, coat with flour, knocking off any excess, and set aside.

Place the butter in a bowl and work with an electric beater or your hands until soft and creamy, then gradually work in the sugar and the vanilla. Mix in the egg whites, one at a time, then fold in the flour.

Drop by teaspoons onto the prepared pan, leaving space for spreading. Bake in a preheated 375° F. oven for 12 to 15 minutes, or until golden brown. Meanwhile, melt the chocolate over hot, not boiling, water.

When cookies are baked, lift off the pan immediately and cool on a cake rack. When cold, lift each cookie up with a needle or fork and dip one side into the melted chocolate. Put back on the rack to dry. Makes about 25.

SNOWBALLS

> Sifted confectioners' sugar (about ¾ cup)
> ⅔ cup coarsely chopped nuts*
> 1 egg white
> Dash of vanilla extract

* Any nuts can be used. Almonds, walnuts, filberts.

Place ½ cup of the sugar and the nuts in a mortar and pound with a pestle, or blend in an electric blender at high speed for 30 seconds. Work in the egg white and the vanilla with a spatula or your hands. This should give you a paste firm enough to roll into balls.

Make little balls with about 1 teaspoon of the paste for each. Roll in confectioners' sugar and place in little paper candy cups, if available, or directly on an ungreased baking sheet. Bake in a preheated 325° to 350° F. oven for 15 to 25 minutes, or until the cookies have puffed up and taken on a nice color. Makes about 12.

NÉGRITAS

1 square (1-ounce size) unsweetened chocolate
½ cup plus ½ tablespoon commercial almond paste
½ teaspoon vanilla extract
3 egg whites
¼ cup sugar
⅓ cup water
1 tablespoon Grand Marnier

Melt the chocolate over hot, not boiling, water and set aside. Combine the almond paste, broken into bits, the vanilla, 1 egg white, the sugar and the water in a bowl. Mix well until smooth, then stir in the melted chocolate.

Beat the remaining whites until stiff enough to stand in peaks. Whip one third of the whites into the chocolate mixture vigorously with a wire whip. Fold in the remainder and the Grand Marnier with a spatula.

Drop by teaspoons onto a greased and lightly floured baking sheet, leaving space for spreading. Bake in a preheated 400° F. oven for 15 to 20 minutes. Makes 25 to 30 cookies.

MACAROONS

¾ cup whole blanched almonds*
1 cup less 2 tablespoons sugar
2 egg whites
Dash of vanilla extract

Grease a baking sheet, coat with flour, dumping off any excess, and set aside.

Blend the almonds with 6 tablespoons of the sugar in the container of the electric blender. When thoroughly blended, combine with the remaining sugar. Work in the egg whites, one at a time, then the vanilla. You should have a soft dough but still firm enough so it won't run.

Spoon the dough into a pastry bag and pipe it onto the prepared pan, making 15 to 18 macaroons. Figure on about 2 tablespoons of the paste for each macaroon. Moisten the tops with a finger dipped into water; sprinkle tops with granulated sugar.

Bake in a preheated 300° to 325° F. oven for about 20 minutes, or until light brown. Lift off the paper and cool the macaroons on a wire rack. Store in an airtight container.

*Commercial almond paste can be used; in this case take one 8-ounce can and combine it with only 3 tablespoons of sugar; then add the egg whites and follow remaining directions.

DÉLICES CAPRICE
(Almond Cookies)

> 1 cup blanched almonds
> 1½ cups sugar
> ∾ 4 egg whites
> ⅓ cup all-purpose flour
> Applesauce
> Apricot Glaze (see Glossary) flavored with
>   kirsch or Cognac
> Slivered toasted almonds

Grease a baking sheet, coat with flour, dumping off any excess, and set aside.

Combine the almonds, sugar and 2 of the egg whites in the container of an electric blender. Blend for 1 minute, or until you have a smooth paste. Fold in the flour.

Beat the remaining whites until stiff enough to stand in peaks when you hold up the beater. Fold into the almond mixture with a wooden spatula carefully but thoroughly.

Drop the mixture by teaspoons onto the prepared baking sheet about 5 inches apart to allow for spreading. You should get about 18 circles or disks, 3 to 4 inches in diameter. Bake in a preheated 375° F. oven for 10 to 12 minutes. When baked, lift off the cookie sheet and cool on wire racks.

To finish the cookies, make sandwiches with 2 tablespoons of applesauce between. Line the "sandwiches" up on a tray and coat the top of each with apricot glaze (see Glossary). Sprinkle tops with slivered toasted almonds. Makes about 16.

~

LANGUES-DE-CHATS
(Cats' Tongues)

> ¼ pound butter
> ½ cup sugar
> Dash of vanilla extract
> ~ 2 egg whites
> ⅓ cup all-purpose flour

Grease baking sheets thoroughly and set aside.

Work the butter until soft and fluffy with an electric beater or your hands. Then work in the sugar gradually, along with the vanilla, until you have a creamy homogeneous mixture. Add the egg whites, one at a time, beating them in thoroughly. Fold in the flour with a wooden spatula.

Fit a pastry bag with a plain, small *douille,* or tube, then fill about two-thirds full with the batter. Press batter out on prepared pans in strips about as thick as a cigarette and 3 inches long, leaving 1 inch between to allow for spreading. Before placing in the oven, give the sheet a good bang on your work table to flatten the cookies.

Bake in a preheated 400° F. oven for 12 minutes, or until light brown. Remove from cookie sheets onto cake racks at once, but allow to dry for at least 45 minutes before using.

Cats' Tongues keep well if stored in a tightly covered tin in a cool place. Makes approximately 45.

Lemon Cats' Tongues: In place of the vanilla, add the grated rind and juice of ½ lemon. Follow the same directions for making and baking.

CIGARETTES

∾ 2 egg whites
3 tablespoons all-purpose flour
4 tablespoons butter, melted
1 cup less 1 tablespoon sugar
Dash of vanilla extract

Grease a baking sheet, coat with flour, knocking off any excess, and set aside.

Beat the egg whites with an electric or rotary beater until they stand in peaks when you hold up the beater. Fold in the flour thoroughly but gently, then stir in all the remaining ingredients. Spoon the batter by tablespoons onto the prepared pan, leaving about 5 inches between the mounds to allow for spreading. Give the pan a good bang on a flat surface to flatten the cigarettes.

Bake in a preheated 375° F. oven for 12 to 15 minutes, or until golden brown. Take out of oven and, while still hot, roll each cookie around a pencil to give it the shape of a cigarette. Allow to dry before using.

Since the cookies dry very fast once they are baked and out of the oven, you must work quickly. If dry, they will break, making them impossible to roll. Makes about 25.

TUILES À L'ORANGE
(Orange Cookies)

½ cup sugar
Dash of vanilla extract
∾ 2 egg whites
⅓ cup all-purpose flour
4 tablespoons butter, melted
½ cup slivered blanched almonds
Grated rind of ½ orange

Butter a baking sheet and set aside.

Combine the sugar, vanilla and egg whites in a bowl and beat with an electric or rotary beater for 1 minute, or until mixture is foaming. Add all the remaining ingredients, mixing them in well.

Drop batter from a coffee spoon onto prepared pans, leaving enough space between mounds to allow for spreading. Bake in preheated 400° F. oven for 10 to 12 minutes. While still hot, lift off baking sheet and bend each cookie over a rolling pin so it takes the shape of a curved roof tile. *Tuiles* should be allowed to dry on the rolling pin long enough to maintain the shape when cold. Makes about 20.

SEÑORITAS

> 1 can (8 ounces), commercial almond paste,
> less 2 tablespoons*
> ¼ cup granulated sugar
> ½ teaspoon vanilla extract
> ⅓ cup water
> 3 egg whites
> ½ cup sifted confectioners' sugar

Grease baking sheets, coat with flour, knocking off any excess, and set aside.

Break up the almond paste into a bowl and combine with the granulated sugar and vanilla. Add the water slowly, beating steadily with a wire whip or electric beater until you have a smooth paste.

Beat the whites until stiff and whip about one third into the almond paste vigorously with a wire whip. Fold in remaining whites with a spatula.

Drop the mixture by teaspoons onto the prepared pans and

* Or ¾ cup whole blanched almonds with 1 cup granulated sugar, ground together in an electric blender.

sprinkle with confectioners' sugar. When cookies are all on baking sheet, hit the sheet on the table to flatten and smooth them out. Bake in a preheated 400° F. oven for 12 to 15 minutes, or until golden brown. Makes 25 to 30.

STRAWBERRY MERINGUES

1 cup sugar
⅓ cup water
¾ cup puréed strawberries (about 1 pint
whole strawberries)
❤ 4 egg whites

Grease baking sheets, coat with flour, knocking off any excess, and set aside.

Mix the sugar with the water. Place over heat, bring to a boil, and cook for about 4 minutes. By that time the syrup should be thick and have reached the "small-crack" stage (300° F. on thermometer). Add the strawberries and let the syrup cook for 8 to 10 minutes, or until it again reaches "small-crack" consistency. Lacking a thermometer, you can determine this by dropping a little syrup into cold water when it should harden and break but still stick to the teeth.

In the meantime, whip the egg whites until they stand in peaks when you lift up the beater. Begin to add the strawberry syrup in a slow steady stream, beating constantly. Without an extra pair of hands, the electric mixer is a godsend at a time like this.

Fill a pastry bag, fitted with a plain or fluted tube, two thirds full with the strawberry mixture and pipe long narrow meringues shaped like ladyfingers (page 193) onto the wax paper. Bake in a preheated 200° to 220° F. oven for 2½ hours. Makes about 25.

These meringues, which are very delicate, can be served with Crème Chantilly (see Glossary), ice cream or fruits.

Extra Whites in ～ ～ ～
Desserts

ANGEL CAKE

> 1 cup sifted confectioners' sugar
> ½ teaspoon salt
> 1 cup sifted cake flour
> ∽ 1½ cups egg whites (11 to 12 whites, depending on size)
> 1 teaspoon almond extract
> 1½ teaspoons cream of tartar
> 1¼ cups superfine sugar

Combine the confectioners' sugar, salt, and cake flour. Then sift twice more. Set aside.

In a very large bowl combine the whites and the almond extract and cream of tartar. Beat with the electric beater, or in a mixer at the highest speed, until whites stand in peaks when you lift up the beater. Add the superfine sugar, a small amount at a time, beating only long enough after each addition to incorporate the sugar.

When all the sugar is in, carefully fold in the flour mixture with a spatula, a spoonful at a time, making sure all the flour is well combined, but folding only until the batter is well blended. Overmixing is fatal to angel cake.

Pour into an ungreased 10-inch tube pan. Bake in the center of a preheated 350° F. oven for 35 minutes, or until cake springs back when touched lightly. Invert the pan on a funnel or over a cake rack. Allow to "hang" until cold. To remove cake from pan, run a sharp thin-bladed knife around side of pan with one long steady stroke and invert cake on serving plate.

CAKE SYLVIA

> 10 squares (1-ounce size) semisweet chocolate
> 　　or 1 package (12-ounce size) semisweet
> 　　chocolate pieces
> 4 ounces whole blanched almonds
> 4 egg whites
> 1 cup sugar
> 2 tablespoons cornstarch

Grease a baking sheet and coat it with flour, dumping off any excess. Mark 3 circles, 7 or 8 inches in diameter, on the floured surface with the point of a knife, using a cake pan as a guide. Set aside.

Melt the chocolate over hot, not boiling, water; grind all except 8 or 10 almonds in the electric blender; chop the 8 or 10 almonds coarsely and set aside.

Place the egg whites in the mixing bowl of an electric mixer and beat until stiff enough to stand in peaks when you lift up the beater. At this point, begin to add the sugar slowly, beating steadily. When all the sugar is in, turn motor to low and add the ground almonds and cornstarch. Place the mixture in a pastry bag. Using a plain tube, pipe out the mixture to cover the 3 circles on the prepared pan with a layer about ½ inch thick.

Bake in a preheated 350° F. oven for 10 to 12 minutes. Take out of the oven and cool on cake racks. Place one meringue round on a serving plate, coat with some of the melted chocolate, place second layer on top, coat again with chocolate, finish with third layer, and coat it with remaining chocolate. Sprinkle chopped almonds over the top and refrigerate until serving time.

BAKED ALASKA

½ recipe for Cake Sylvia (preceding recipe)
⌒ 3 egg whites
⅓ cup sugar
1 quart hard coffee ice cream*

Line a baking sheet with buttered wax paper. With a pencil mark an oval 10 inches long and 5 inches wide at the widest point, using whatever you have at hand as a guide. Make the meringue base from the Cake Sylvia recipe, making only half of the recipe. Spoon the meringue into a pastry bag, fitted with a plain tube, and pipe over the oval on the prepared pan. Bake in a preheated 350° F. oven for 15 to 20 minutes. Cool.

Whip the 3 egg whites until stiff when you hold up the beater, then begin to add the sugar, little by little, until all is used. Once all the sugar has been incorporated, beat at high speed (if using an electric beater or mixer) for 45 seconds.

Place the ice cream in the center of the cooled meringue oval. Cover with three fourths of the meringue, smoothing the meringue with a spatula and making sure the ice cream is completely "insulated." Spoon the remaining meringue into a pastry bag fitted with a fluted tube and decorate the top. Sprinkle with confectioners' sugar.

Bake in a preheated 450° F. oven for 3 to 4 minutes, or until meringue is tinged with gold. Serve immediately to 8 or, even 10.

* Any flavor of ice cream may be used.

OEUFS À LA NEIGE AU CHOCOLAT
(Chocolate Floating Island)

> 1 quart milk
> Dash of vanilla extract
> 3 egg whites
> 1½ cups sugar, in all
> 2½ squares (1-ounce size) unsweetened
> chocolate
> 4 tablespoons butter
> 1½ tablespoons flour
> ½ cup toasted slivered almonds

Combine the milk and vanilla in a shallow heavy saucepan; bring to a boil.

Whip the egg whites with a rotary or electric beater, or in an electric mixer, until they stand in peaks when you hold up the beater. Then add 6 tablespoons of the sugar gradually, beating steadily. (If you are using an electric mixer, dump this amount of sugar in all at one time, turn beater to high, and beat for 1 minute.) Add 6 more tablespoons of the sugar, again slowly, beating constantly. (In mixer, beat at low speed for 2 or 3 minutes.) Using a big spoon, take enough of the beaten whites to make into an egg shape and drop the "egg" into the simmering milk. Make 4 or 5 more and add to the milk. Poach without boiling for 2½ minutes on one side, then turn with a wooden spatula and poach for the same length of time on the other. Lift out of milk with a slotted spoon, drain on paper towels, then refrigerate. Make another batch of "eggs" with the remaining whites.

Add the chocolate to simmering milk. Work butter, remaining ¾ cup sugar and the flour together well. When chocolate has melted, stir in the butter-sugar mixture and bring to a boil, stirring constantly; boil for 1 minute. Strain custard through a fine sieve or several layers of cheesecloth. Place a piece of Saran directly on top of the custard to prevent skin forming. Refrigerate until cold.

At serving time, pour chocolate custard into a handsome bowl. Stick the slivered almonds into the "eggs" and arrange them on top of the chocolate custard. Serve very cold. Serves 8.

MERINGUES CHANTILLY

∽ 4 egg whites
1 cup granulated sugar
7 tablespoons sifted confectioners' sugar
2 cups heavy cream
Dash of vanilla extract
Powdered cocoa or granulated sugar

Grease 2 cookie sheets and coat with flour, knocking off any excess. Set aside.

Place the egg whites in a medium-sized bowl and beat with an electric or rotary beater until they begin to hold a shape, about 3 minutes. At this point sprinkle half of the granulated sugar over the surface of the whites and continue beating hard (at high speed, if you are using an electric beater or mixer) for about 1 minute. Add remaining granulated sugar gradually while constantly beating, allowing it to fall slowly onto the whites "like rain." The finished meringue should be very shiny and stiff enough to stand in peaks when you hold up the beater. "Wet," as the saying goes, but not dry.

Spoon the meringue into a pastry bag fitted with a No. 7 tube and press out oval shells 1½ inches wide and 4 inches long. Sprinkle with confectioners' sugar. This amount of meringue should yield about 24 shells, to serve 10 or 12.

Bake in a preheated 200° F. oven for 2½ to 3 hours. Correctly, the baked shells should be pure white, but if your oven isn't constant, they may turn a pale yellow. Once you take them from the oven, lift with a spatula from the wax paper immediately and cool on wire racks.

Whip the cream until it begins to hold a shape, add remaining confectioners' sugar and the vanilla, and continue to whip until the cream is stiff. Take care not to overwhip, otherwise your cream will become granular and turn to butter. Spoon the cream into a pastry bag. To serve, press about 3 tablespoons of the cream onto the flat side of a meringue shell, put another shell on top, and sprinkle top with a little shower of cocoa or sugar.

VACHERIN AUX FRAISES
(Meringue with Strawberries and Cream)

> Meringues (see Meringues Chantilly, opposite), for which you need 4 egg whites
> 1 pint strawberries
> Crème Chantilly (see Glossary)

Grease 2 baking sheets and coat completely with flour, dumping off any excess. Using any 6-inch circle as a guide, mark off several circles on the floured pans and set aside.

Make meringue as in Meringues Chantilly. Fit a pastry bag with a plain tube and fill the bag about two thirds full with the meringue. Pipe a layer of the meringue about ½ inch thick on one of the circles, covering the entire circle. With the remaining meringue, make 6-inch rings ½ inch wide and ½ inch thick until all the meringue is used up. Bake circle and rings in a preheated 200° F. oven for 2½ to 3 hours.

While meringues bake, wash the strawberries, drain well on paper towels, then hull. Refrigerate.

Shortly before serving, make crème Chantilly. Spoon the cream into a pastry bag fitted with a fluted tube and pipe over the surface of the meringue circle. Place one of the rings on top and pipe more cream on top of the ring. Continue until all rings are used. Combine the strawberries and the remainder of the cream and spoon the mixture into center of the *vacherin*. Refrigerate until ready to serve. Serves 10.

MONT BLANC
(Chestnut Purée with Meringues)

> 20 meringues (see Meringues Chantilly, page
> ~ 148), for which you need 4 egg whites
> 1½ pounds chestnuts
> 3 cups milk
> Dash of vanilla extract
> ¼ pound butter, softened
> 1 cup granulated sugar
> 1 cup water
> Crème Chantilly (see Glossary)

Make the meringues as in Meringues Chantilly.

With a sharp knife, make an incision on the flat side of each chestnut. Drop the nuts into boiling water for 5 minutes, then peel while still warm. Place in a saucepan with the milk and vanilla and cook over moderate heat until tender, about 45 minutes.

Push the chestnuts through a fine sieve to make a very compact and smooth purée. Mix in the softened butter thoroughly. Combine the granulated sugar with the water and bring to a boil over moderate heat, stirring constantly until sugar has dissolved; boil for 8 minutes. Stir the hot syrup into the chestnut mixture. Taste for sweetness. If not sweet enough according to your taste, add a bit more sugar. Make the crème Chantilly.

To compose the Mont Blanc, spoon 2 or 3 tablespoons of the chestnut purée on a meringue, cover with a second meringue, and pipe crème Chantilly over the top. Serves 10.

COCONUT SNOW

> 3 egg whites
> 3 tablespoons sifted confectioners' sugar
> 1 cup heavy cream
> 1 tablespoon rosewater
> 2 cans (4-ounce size) flaked coconut

Beat the egg whites until they stand in peaks, then beat in the sugar, 1 tablespoon at a time. Whip the cream until very stiff but not granular, then fold in the rosewater. Carefully fold the beaten whites into the cream with a spatula.

Heap the coconut in the center of a crystal or silver serving bowl and spoon the "snow" over it. This must be done at the last minute because the delicate egg and cream mixture will not hold up for any length of time. Garnish with candied rose petals. Serves 4.

CHOCOLATE MOUSSE

> 4 egg whites
> Dash of cream of tartar
> 1 cup plus 1 tablespoon sugar
> 8 squares (1-ounce size) semisweet chocolate
>   or 1½ packages (6-ounce size) semisweet
>   chocolate pieces
> ¼ pound plus 2 tablespoons butter, softened
> 1½ envelopes unflavored gelatin
> ¾ cup cold water

Beat the egg whites and the cream of tartar with an electric or rotary beater until stiff enough to stand in peaks when you hold up the beater. Add the sugar, little by little, beating constantly until all the sugar is incorporated and the meringue stands in stiff shiny peaks.

Melt the chocolate over hot, not boiling, water. Take off the heat and stir in the softened butter. Sprinkle the gelatin over the cold water in a saucepan. Place over low heat and stir until dissolved. When dissolved, add to the chocolate and butter, and beat until mixture has reached room tempearture (in short, the same temperature as the meringue). Fold in the meringue, spoon into a mold, and refrigerate for at least 3 hours. Serves 8 to 10.

~ NOTE: Chocolate Mousse will keep for several days if refrigerated.

PORT-WINE CREAM

> ¼ pound sweet butter
> 2 cups sifted confectioners' sugar
> Strained juice of 1 lemon
> ¼ cup port wine
> 2 tablespoons Cognac
> ~ 2 egg whites, beaten
> 1 cup heavy cream, whipped
> Freshly grated nutmeg

Cream the butter until soft, then work in the sugar gradually until the mixture is smooth and fluffy. Gradually beat in the lemon juice, beating constantly and hard. Combine the wine and Cognac, then dribble into the mixture, beating constantly. Fold the beaten whites in, followed by the whipped cream. Pile in a crystal serving bowl, dust lightly with the nutmeg, and chill slightly before serving. Serves 6.

*T*ANGERINE SHERBET

> 5 tangerines
> 2 cups sugar
> 1½ cups water
> 1 small glass of orange liqueur or Grand Marnier
> ½ recipe for Meringue Italienne (page 163), for which you need 2 egg whites

Peel the rind off 3 of the tangerines. Blanch the rind for 1 minute in boiling water, then rinse under cold water. Place in a heavy saucepan with 1½ cups of the sugar and the water. Stir constantly over moderate heat until syrup comes to a boil and the sugar is dissolved. Boil, without stirring, for 4 minutes, or until a thermometer reaches 200° to 210° F. Cool.

Peel the remaining tangerines, section, then squeeze out the juice. This is best done in a food mill, but it can also be done by working the fruit through a fine sieve. Strain the juice, combine with the cold syrup and the liqueur.

Pour into the container of an electric freezer, packed with layers of crushed ice and coarse salt. Freeze for 15 to 20 minutes, or until sherbet is about three-fourths done. At this point, stir in the Meringue Italienne and freeze for another 15 minutes. Spoon into a mold and place in the freezer or the freezing compartment of the refrigerator.

Like all "water" ices, this sherbet melts very quickly once it is taken from the freezer, so keep this in mind when it is served. Serves 10.

PRUNE WHIP

    1 cup dried prunes
    ¼ cup sugar
    1 teaspoon vanilla extract
    ½ cup coarsely chopped walnuts
 ∽ 5 egg whites
    Whipped cream

Prepare a 2-quart baking dish or casserole, coating it with granulated sugar (page 203).
 Cover the prunes with water and cook until tender when
tested with a fork. Drain, remove the pits, and chop the prunes
very fine. You should have 1 cupful. Mix together with the sugar,
vanilla, and chopped nuts.
 Beat the egg whites until they hold a definite point, then fold
gently into the prune mixture.
 Pour into the prepared baking dish and bake in a preheated
375° F. oven for 20 to 25 minutes, or until delicately browned.
Serve with whipped cream. Serves 6.

APPLES IN MERINGUE

    6 apples
    6 large lumps sugar
    ¼ pound butter
    ½ cup water
 ∽ 2 egg whites
    ½ cup granulated sugar

Core the apples carefully. Place a sugar lump in the center of each
and a generous tablespoon of the butter. Arrange in a baking pan,
add the water, and bake in a preheated 400° F. oven for 25
minutes. Cool.

Beat the egg whites with a rotary or electric beater until they begin to take shape. Gradually add the granulated sugar, beating constantly until meringue stands in peaks when you hold up the beater.

Place the cooled apples in an ovenproof serving dish. Spoon the meringue into a pastry bag fitted with a fluted tube, and cover each of the apples completely.

Bake in a preheated 400° F. oven for 10 to 12 minutes, or until the meringue is delicately brown. Serve hot or cold. Serves 6.

APRICOT OR ORANGE MERINGUE SOUFFLÉ

½ cup slivered toasted almonds, ground
6 egg whites
⅛ teaspoon salt
⅛ teaspoon cream of tartar
¼ cup sugar
¼ cup apricot jam*
Apricot Glaze (see Glossary)

Prepare a 2-quart soufflé dish (page 203) coating it with some of the ground almonds. Refrigerate.

Beat the egg whites until just foamy, then beat in the salt and cream of tartar. Continue beating until the whites are shiny and hold firm peaks when you hold the beater straight up. Stir the sugar and jam together. Add this to the whites very gradually, beating constantly, until the mixture is very stiff. Spoon into the prepared soufflé dish and sprinkle the remaining ground almonds over the top. Place in a pan with enough hot water to reach to half the depth of the dish, and bake in a preheated 325° F. oven for 45 minutes. Serve the apricot glaze as a sauce.

*Orange marmalade can be substituted in the same amount, in which case serve with Orange Custard Sauce, page 110.

TARTE AUX POIRES
(Pear Tart)

Pastry for a 9-inch, 1-crust pie*
4 fresh firm pears
¼ pound butter
1½ cups sugar, in all
Grated rind of ½ lemon
2 egg whites

Make the pastry and use it to line a 9-inch pie pan. Refrigerate.

Peel the pears and slice fairly thin. Melt the butter in a heavy skillet, add the pear slices, and sprinkle with 1 cup of the sugar. Add the lemon rind and sauté for 4 or 5 minutes. Cool.

When cold, arrange the pear slices in the pastry-lined pan. Bake in a preheated 400° F. oven for 35 minutes or until pastry is golden. Take out of the oven and cool.

Beat the egg whites until they stand in peaks when you hold up the beater, add the remaining ½ cup sugar gradually, and continue beating until the meringue is stiff and shiny.

Spread the meringue on the pears right to the edge of the pastry, making sure meringue touches the pastry all around. Place the tart in a preheated 350° F. oven for 5 to 8 minutes, or until the meringue is flecked with gold. If you wish, you may pipe the meringue onto the pie and make fancy decorations. In that case, use a fluted pastry tube. Serves 6 to 8.

* Pastry recipe for Galette au Citron (page 102) or your own.

TARTE AU RIZ SOUFFLÉ
(Rice Soufflé Tart)

Pastry for a 9-inch, 1-crust pie*
2 cups milk
⅓ cup uncooked long-grain rice
¼ cup raisins
½ cup sugar
½ teaspoon grated lemon rind
Few drops of vanilla extract
3 egg whites

Make the pastry and use it to line a 9-inch pie pan. Refrigerate.

Scald the milk in the top of a double boiler. Add the rice and stir until grains have separated. Cook, covered, for 1 hour, stirring occasionally.

Meanwhile, pick over the raisins to eliminate any seeds or stray stems. Cover raisins with water and let them stand to plump up. When the rice is cooked, stir into it the sugar, well-drained raisins, lemon rind and vanilla. Cook for 4 or 5 minutes longer. Take off the stove and cool slightly.

Beat egg whites with a rotary or electric beater until they stand in peaks when you lift up the beater. Fold the beaten whites into the cooled rice mixture. Pour into the pastry-lined pan. Bake in a preheated 425° F. oven for 15 to 20 minutes, or until the pastry is golden brown. Serves 6 to 8.

* Use pastry recipe for Galette au Citron (page 102) or your own.

LIME CHIFFON PIE

> 12 graham crackers
> 3 tablespoons butter, melted
> Grated rind of 1 lime
> ½ cup lime juice (several limes)
> 3 tablespoons cornstarch
> 1½ cups boiling water
> ∾ 3 egg whites
> ½ cup sugar

Roll the graham crackers into fine crumbs, then mix thoroughly with the melted butter until crumbs hold together. Pat onto bottom and around sides of a 9-inch pie plate. Bake in a preheated 350° F. oven for about 7 minutes. Cool while you make the filling.

Mix the rind and the juice of the limes with the cornstarch. Stir this mixture into the boiling water slowly and cook, stirring constantly, for about 5 minutes, or until liquid is clear. Take off the heat.

Beat the egg whites until they begin to take a shape. Then add the sugar gradually, beating constantly until the meringue is smooth and shiny. Add the cornstarch mixture to the meringue very slowly, folding it in gently until all patches of white have disappeared. Pour into the baked shell and chill in refrigerator until firm. Serves 6 to 8.

STRAWBERRY CHIFFON PIE

  1 baked 9-inch pastry shell*
  ½ cup milk
  1 envelope unflavored gelatin
  1 package (10 ounces) frozen sliced
    strawberries in syrup, thawed
  3 egg whites
  Dash of salt
  ¼ teaspoon cream of tartar
  ¼ cup sugar
  1 cup heavy cream, whipped

Pour the milk into a large saucepan and sprinkle gelatin over the top. Place over low heat for 3 to 5 minutes, stirring constantly until the gelatin has dissolved. Take off the heat and stir in the strawberries. Chill in the refrigerator until the mixture begins to take a shape when dropped from a spoon.

Beat the egg whites with the salt and cream of tartar until whites stand in peaks when you hold up the beater. Add sugar gradually, a small amount at a time, beating until the mixture is stiff and shiny. Fold into the gelatin mixture gently but thoroughly, then fold in the whipped cream. Spoon into the pastry shell and chill until firm. Serves 6 to 8.

* Pastry recipe for Galette au Citron (page 102) or your own.

ALMOND PUDDING

  1 cup whole blanched almonds
  ½ cup sugar
  3 tablespoons water
  2 tablespoons Cognac or rum
  4 egg whites
  Dash of salt
  Chocolate Glaze (see Glossary)

Butter generously a 6-inch springform pan or a similar dessert mold. Grind the almonds in the electric blender or put through a food mill.

Combine the sugar with the water, place over moderate heat, and stir until dissolved. Add the ground almonds and cook over very low heat, stirring constantly with a wooden spatula, until the mixture forms a ball in the center of the pan. Take care not to let the mixture scorch. Take off the heat and cool. When cold (at this point it will be hard), grind in the blender or pound in a mortar until very fine. Pour into a bowl and work in the Cognac or rum. Beat the egg whites and the salt with an electric or rotary beater until they stand in peaks. Fold in the ground nuts carefully but thoroughly.

Pour into the buttered pan, then set the pan in another pan with enough boiling water added to reach to a depth of about two thirds of the pudding pan.

It will probably be necessary to put a weight on the pudding pan so it will not float in the water. You will simply have to use your own ingenuity here, but you must not completely cover the pudding. Place in the center of a preheated 300° F. oven and bake for 1 hour and 10 minutes, or until a food pick plunged in the center comes out dry. Cool.

Make the chocolate glaze. Turn the pudding out of the mold and pour chocolate glaze over the top and smooth around the sides. Cool.

To serve this odd but interesting pudding, cut it into small wedges. Serves 4 to 6.

Extra Whites in ~ ~ ~
Frostings

ORNAMENTAL FROSTING

> ∾　2 egg whites
> 2½ cups sifted confectioners' sugar
> 5 drops of lemon extract

Place egg whites in a mixing bowl and add the sugar gradually, working it in well with a rubber or wooden spatula; this can also be done in an electric mixer or with an electric beater. When all the sugar is in, add the lemon extract. Continue to mix or beat until you have a smooth shiny mixture, but do not overbeat or frosting will become too hard to work with.

To ice a cake, pour frosting on the center of the cake and spread it out with a rubber spatula. Makes 2 cups, or enough to frost a 2-layer, 8-inch cake.

STRAWBERRY FROSTING

> ∾　1 egg white
> 1 cup mashed strawberries
> 1 cup sifted confectioners' sugar
> 2 tablespoons butter, softened

Beat the egg white until it stands in peaks. Combine with the strawberries and continue beating until mixture looks fluffy. Gradually beat in the sugar and the softened butter, beating until sauce is light and airy. Makes about 2 cups.

Serve over fresh cakes, small or large, or decorate a strawberry shortcake with it.

COFFEE MERINGUE CREAM

2 egg whites
⅔ cup sugar
2 tablespoons powdered instant coffee
½ pound sweet butter, softened

Beat the egg whites with an electric beater or in an electric mixer until they begin to take shape; then gradually beat in the sugar. Continue beating until meringue stands in peaks when you hold up the beater. Then fold in the coffee.

Add the softened butter, bit by bit, beating at low speed, taking care not to overbeat or cream will separate. When all the butter is in, refrigerate.

This cream is used primarily to decorate cakes.

MERINGUE ITALIENNE

1 cup sugar
½ cup water
4 egg whites
Pinch of salt

Mix the sugar with the water in a saucepan. Stir over moderate heat until sugar has dissolved and syrup comes to a boil. Boil gently, without stirring, for 8 to 10 minutes. At this point you should have a foamy mixture which is still clear and white, the stage known in the professional kitchen as *petit cassé,* which is just before the sugar begins to caramelize.

About 4 minutes after syrup has begun to boil, place the egg whites and salt in the electric mixer and begin whipping on medium speed. Just before you are ready to add the syrup, turn mixer to high for 15 to 20 seconds. The whites should be white, fluffy and stiff, not granular or "dry." Reduce speed to medium, and begin to add the syrup in a steady stream. When all the syrup has been added, continue beating for 5 or 6 more minutes. The meringue should be very white, shiny and smooth. Spoon into a clean bowl, cover tightly, and refrigerate until needed.

Meringue Italienne is used in place of whipped cream to decorate tarts, in Tangerine Sherbert (page 153), etc.

BOILED FROSTING

1½ cups sugar
¼ teaspoon cream of tartar
Salt
½ cup corn syrup
½ cup water
~ 4 egg whites

Mix the sugar, cream of tartar, a pinch of salt, the corn syrup and water in a heavy skillet. Place over moderate heat and stir until sugar has dissolved and mixture comes to a boil. Boil, without stirring, for 5 minutes, or until the syrup reaches 232° F. on a thermometer.

Beat the egg whites with a pinch of salt in an electric mixer until they stand in peaks when you hold up the beater. Begin to add the syrup in a thin steady stream. When all the syrup is incorporated, set the mixer on medium speed, beating constantly for 20 minutes. The frosting should be very white, shiny, rather stiff and sticky.

Although it is easier to spread the frosting when it is freshly made, it is possible to store this frosting, securely covered, in the refrigerator for several days, or even to freeze it. If frozen, it should be brought to room temperature gradually.

Makes enough to frost a 2-layer, 8- to 9-inch cake.

PART IV

Eggs and Their Other Halves
in ∽ ∽ ∽

Some Special Dishes

Desserts

Soufflés

Eggs and Their Other Halves in ⌒ ⌒ ⌒

Some Special Dishes

One way to use up yolks or whites is simply to pitch in and use still more—whole—eggs. Here one gets into egg cookery per se, which is not the primary purpose of this book. But nothing gets along so well with either half of the egg as the egg itself. So the three sections of our Part IV include some egg dishes as well as desserts and—the crowning glory of all egg cookery—soufflés. All the recipes use whole eggs plus either extra yolks or extra whites.

CAMEMBERT CROQUETTES

½ cup sifted all-purpose flour
⅜ pound butter (1½ sticks)
4 ounces Camembert cheese
Pinch of cayenne
Pinch of paprika
⌒ 2 extra egg yolks
Fat for deep frying
⌒ 1 whole egg
Fine dry bread crumbs

Combine the flour, butter, cheese, cayenne and paprika in a mixing bowl. Work together with a pastry blender, 2 knives or your fingers until mixture looks and feels mealy. Beat the egg yolks slightly, then knead into the mixture with the heel of your hand until the pastry holds together. Refrigerate for 2 hours at least.

Roll out on a lightly floured board into a sheet about ½ inch thick, then cut into attractive shapes—small squares, oblongs or circles.

Preheat the fat to 350° F. on a thermometer, or until hot enough to brown a small cube of bread in 1 minute. Beat the whole egg very well. Dip the pieces of pastry into the egg, then coat with the crumbs. Fry in the hot fat until crisp and golden. Drain on paper towels. Serve piping hot as an hors-d'oeuvre.

EGGS VINAIGRETTE

~ 6 hard-cooked eggs
1 can (2 ounces) anchovy fillets
1 recipe Rich Vinaigrette (page 98)
~ for which you need 1 egg yolk

Halve the eggs lengthwise and place 2 anchovy fillets crosswise over each half. Arrange eggs on a serving dish and spoon the sauce over them. Serves. 4

This makes an interesting appetizer.

EGGS IN ASPIC

> Aspic (next page), for which you need
>   8 egg whites
> Fresh tarragon leaves
> 6 tender eggs (*oeufs mollets,* page 21),
>   cooled
> Thin slices of ham
> Watercress

Pour a thin layer of the liquid aspic into the bottom of 6 round or oval ½-cup metal molds or custard cups. Refrigerate until set. Pour more aspic into a bowl and chill until syrupy.

Blanch the tarragon leaves in boiling water, then refresh in cold water. Drain, dry and chill. When cold, dip the leaves into the syrupy aspic and arrange them in a design on top of the set jelly in each mold. Chill briefly to set the tarragon leaves.

Place 1 tender egg in each mold and cover with a slice of ham cut in a round or oval to fit. Gently pour in enough of the almost-set jelly to fill the mold. Chill the molds and the remaining aspic until firm. Chop the remaining firm aspic into tiny dice.

To serve, dip the bottom of each mold into hot water for 3 or 4 seconds. Run a knife around the edge of the jelly and turn upside down on a serving platter. Give the mold a sharp tap if the egg doesn't drop out easily.

Garnish with a bouquet of watercress and a garland of chopped aspic. Serves 6 as an appetizer.

ASPIC

¾ cup chopped celery leaves
¾ cup chopped green leaves of leeks
½ cup coarsely chopped parsley
¾ cup sliced carrots
2 garlic cloves, unpeeled
1 medium onion, halved, each half stuck
   with 1 clove
Dash of ground thyme
3 bay leaves
1 tablespoon dried tarragon or 2 tablespoons
   coarsely chopped fresh tarragon
¼ teaspoon whole white peppercorns, crushed
2 ripe fresh tomatoes, coarsely chopped
1 tablespoon salt
12 envelopes unflavored gelatin
8 egg whites
2 cups cold water
4 cups canned beef or condensed chicken
   broth, heated

Combine all the ingredients in a heavy kettle and mix well. Bring the mixture to a boil over moderate heat, stirring constantly. Reduce heat to low and simmer for 25 to 30 minutes only. Take off the heat and strain through a fine sieve or several layers of cheesecloth wrung out in cold water. Add a few drops of caramel coloring (available in fancy food shops) to turn the jelly a light gold.

Refrigerate in immaculately clean jars, covered securely, until ready to use. Aspic will keep for several days in refrigerator. Makes 5 cups.

Aspic is used to finish many cold dishes such as pâtés, eggs, fowl, fish, meat, mousses, etc.

BEEF OR CHICKEN CONSOMMÉ
with Royal Custard Garnish

Consommé is a beef or chicken decoction that, when perfectly made, is beautifully clear and sparkling. Ideally, it is made with homemade stock but, for the sake of expediency, this recipe calls for canned beef or chicken broth. Clarification is a simple process but it demands stock and equipment that are absolutely free of any grease. Even a miniscule amount of fat can cloud the finished consommé.

1 pound ground beef, free of fat
⅓ cup coarsely chopped parsley
½ cup chopped celery leaves
½ cup coarsely chopped leek tops
¾ cup sliced carrots
1 large tomato, coarsely chopped
1 medium onion, halved, each half stuck with 2 cloves
1 garlic clove, unpeeled
½ teaspoon salt (about, depending on saltiness of stock)
Dash of dried thyme
3 bay leaves
6 egg whites
3 cups cold water
4 cups canned beef or condensed chicken broth
Caramel coloring (available in fancy food shops)
Royal Custard (next page), for which you need 2 whole eggs and 2 extra egg yolks

In a large skillet mix together, by hand, all the ingredients except the beef or chicken broth, the coloring and the custard garnish. Heat the broth and pour it over the mixed ingredients, stirring with a spoon until well mixed. Bring to a rolling boil over high heat, stirring constantly. Boil, still stirring, for a few seconds.

Reduce heat to simmer. As the mixture simmers, you will notice the ingredients form a "crust" on the surface of the liquid with one or two holes breaking it, through which the liquid boils lightly. Allow the consommé to simmer gently for 1 hour without disturbing the little "geysers" in any way. If the crust which is held by the egg whites is broken, it will not clear the consommé further. After 1 hour, add a few drops of caramel coloring to the consommé through one of the little openings—just enough to turn it a light gold.

When finished, strain the consommé through a very fine sieve or several layers of cheesecloth wrung out in cold water, taking care not to disturb the crust more than necessary. Refrigerated in jars, securely covered, the consommé will keep for 5 to 6 days. Makes 4 to 5 cups. Serve with small cubes of royal custard.

ROYAL CUSTARD

> ~ 2 whole eggs
> ~ 2 extra egg yolks
> ½ cup heavy cream or consommé
> Salt
> Freshly ground white pepper

Whip the whole eggs and egg yolks together until light and fluffy. Stir in the cream or consommé and season to taste with salt and pepper. Pour into a small buttered pan and set the pan in a vessel of hot water.

Bake in a preheated 300° F. oven for 15 to 20 minutes, or until firm. Refrigerate.

To use, cut into fancy shapes and serve as a garnish in hot consommé.

EGGS BENEDICT

Sauté slices of ham lightly in butter. Place each slice on half of a toasted and buttered English muffin. Crown with freshly poached eggs (page 27). Cover with one half recipe for Hollandaise Sauce (page 87) for which you need 2 egg yolks, and garnish with a thin slice of truffle. It is customary to serve 2 eggs to each person.

EGGS HUSSARDE

> 4 Holland rusks
> 4 thin slices of ham, grilled
> ½ cup Marchand de Vins Sauce (see Glossary)
> 4 slices of tomato, grilled
> 4 soft poached eggs (page 27)
> ½ recipe for Hollandaise Sauce (page 87),
>   for which you need 2 egg yolks
> Paprika

Place the rusks on a hot serving plate, lay the slices of ham on top, and cover with marchand de vins sauce. Top with the grilled tomato slices and the poached eggs. Spoon Hollandaise over the eggs and sprinkle with paprika. Serves 2.

EGGS SARDOU

> 2 cups creamed spinach
> 4 cooked artichoke bottoms, sautéed in
>   butter
> 4 poached eggs (page 27)
> ½ recipe for Hollandaise Sauce (page 87),
>   for which you need 2 egg yolks

Make a base of piping hot spinach on a serving plate or in a ramekin. Arrange the artichoke bottoms on top and place a poached egg on each one. Spoon Hollandaise over the eggs. Serves 2.

OEUFS À LA BEAUMANIÈRE
(Eggs and Seafood in Patty Shells)

1 cup ground cooked salmon, lobster or shrimps
⅓ cup Sauce Crème (see Glossary)
6 patty shells, heated
∾ 6 poached eggs (page 27)
½ recipe for Hollandaise Sauce (page 87),
∾ for which you need 2 egg yolks
¼ cup sour cream
⅓ cup grated Gruyère cheese

Work the salmon, lobster or shrimp through a food mill, or blend, a small amount at a time, in an electric blender, until you have a smooth purée. Stir in the hot sauce crème. Spoon the mixture into the hot patty shells and arrange the shells on a baking sheet. Place the poached eggs, neatly trimmed, on top of the purée.

Combine the Hollandaise with the sour cream and spoon over the poached eggs. Sprinkle with the grated Gruyère. Place in a preheated broiler for 1 or 2 minutes, until the cheese has melted and the sauce has browned slightly. Serves 6.

OEUFS À LA CHIMAY
(Eggs with Sauce Mornay)

> 6 hard-cooked eggs
> 5 tablespoons butter, in all
> 1 tablespoon olive oil
> 1 tablespoon minced onion
> ¼ pound mushrooms, finely chopped
> 2 tablespoons tomato purée
> Several sprigs parsley, chopped
> ½ teaspoon salt
> Pepper
> Sauce Mornay (page 84), for which
> you need 3 egg yolks

Cut the hard-cooked eggs lengthwise into halves. Lift the yolks out carefully so as not to break the whites, and mash together the yolks and 4 tablespoons of the butter until smooth.

Melt 1 tablespoon of butter in a skillet, add the oil, and sauté the onion over moderate heat until limp but not brown. Stir in the mushrooms, increase the heat slightly, and cook for 2 or 3 minutes. Add the tomato purée, parsley, salt, and pepper to taste.

Take off the heat and mix in the mashed yolks very thoroughly. Fill the whites with the mushroom mixture and place in a greased baking dish.

Make the sauce Mornay and spoon it over the stuffed eggs.

Place in a preheated 425° F. oven and bake for 5 to 6 minutes—actually, just long enough to heat the eggs. Serves 3 or 4.

SEAFOOD MOUSSE WITH LOBSTER SAUCE

Court Bouillon (see below)
1 lobster (2½ pounds)
½ pound raw shrimps
1 pound sole fillets
¼ pound crabmeat
~ 3 egg whites
¼ cup Cognac
1½ cups heavy cream
1 teaspoon salt
Dash of powdered thyme
Dash of freshly ground white pepper
Dash of cayenne

Court Bouillon

1 onion, cut in two
2 celery stalks, with leaves, coarsely chopped
1 carrot, cut in two
Good pinch of dried thyme
1 bay leaf
Few peppercorns, crushed
1 tablespoon salt
3 quarts cold water

Combine all the ingredients in a large kettle, bring to a boil slowly, then boil for 10 minutes. The court bouillon is now ready for the lobsters to be cooked in it.

Lobster Sauce

> 3 tablespoons butter
> 3 tablespoons flour
> 1 cup lobster broth (above)
> 1 cup light cream
> Juice of ½ lemon
> 1 egg yolk
> Half the lobster meat, diced
> Salt
> Freshly ground white pepper
> Cayenne
> Lobster tomalley and coral, if any
> ¼ cup dry sherry

Plunge the lobster head first into the boiling court bouillon, cover, and cook for 8 minutes after the liquid comes to a boil again. After 3 minutes add the shrimps. When 8 minutes have elapsed, lift both lobster and shrimps out of the broth.

When the shellfish are cool enough to handle, remove the meat from the lobster as well as the liver (green tomalley) and coral (the roe) and toss the empty shells into the kettle with the broth; shell and devein the shrimps. Cut shrimps and lobster meat into small pieces, reserving half of the lobster pieces for the sauce.

Place the kettle with the court bouillon and the empty shells over high heat and reduce until you have 1 cup of concentrated broth. Strain through a fine sieve or several layers of dampened cheesecloth and set aside for the sauce.

Purée the sole, crabmeat, shrimps and half of the lobster pieces —about one third at a time—in the electric blender along with the egg whites, Cognac and ½ cup of the heavy cream until you have a smooth creamy mixture. Turn the purée into a large bowl and mix in the seasonings thoroughly. Then add the remaining cup of cream in a slow steady stream, stirring constantly with a wooden spatula. (If you have an electric mixer, place mousse mixture in the bowl and beat at medium speed, adding the cream slowly.)

Spoon the mousse into a buttered 5-cup ring mold and smooth the top. Set the mold in a pan of hot water. Bake in a preheated 250° F. oven for 35 minutes, or until top is firm to the touch.

Meanwhile, make the lobster sauce. Melt the butter in the top of a double boiler, stir in the flour, and cook for a minute or two. Add the reserved lobster broth and the light cream and cook over moderate heat, stirring with a wire whip, until sauce has thickened. Stir in the lemon juice. Beat the egg yolk slightly, beat in a little of the hot sauce, then combine the two, whipping briskly. Add the reserved lobster meat, seasonings to taste, and the tomalley and coral, if any. At this point, do not cook further, but keep warm over hot, not boiling, water. Just before serving stir in the sherry.

When it is done, turn the mousse out onto a warm serving platter, spoon half of the lobster sauce over the ring, and serve the remainder in a sauceboat. Serves 6.

~ NOTE: The mousse can be made early in the day and refrigerated, but it should be brought to room temperature before baking. Allow 2 hours.

CHICKEN-LIVER TIMBALES

1 cup Sauce Béchamel*
½ pound fresh chicken livers
2 whole eggs
2 extra egg yolks
Dash of freshly ground white pepper
Dash of salt
6 tablespoons heavy cream
2 tablespoons Cognac
Sauce Allemande (page 84), for which
you need 3 extra egg yolks

Make the sauce Béchamel. When cooked, place a piece of Saran right on top to prevent a skin forming. Set the sauce aside to cool.

Cut the livers into small pieces. Place in the electric blender with the eggs, yolks, pepper and salt, and blend at high speed for 1 minute. Add the cooled sauce Béchamel, the cream and Cognac. Blend only until smooth, about 15 seconds. Pour into 8 well-buttered ½-cup ramekins or other small molds.

Set the molds on a rack in a pan of hot water, and bake in a preheated 350° F. oven for 25 to 35 minutes, or until firm. To serve, run a knife around the edge of each timbale and unmold onto a warm serving platter. Spoon a little of the sauce Allemande over each timbale and serve the remainder in a sauceboat. Serves 4.

* Make the Sauce Béchamel (see Glossary) in these proportions: 1½ tablespoons butter, 2 tablespoons flour, and 1 cup milk. Season with salt and freshly ground white pepper.

BLANQUETTE DE VEAU, FAÇON BELGE
(Veal Stew Belgian Style)

⅜ pound butter (1½ sticks)
2½ pounds leg of veal, cut into 1½-inch cubes
2 cups chicken or beef broth
Good pinch of dried thyme
1 bay leaf
12 shallots or the bulbs from 12 scallions,
 coarsely chopped
Good dash of grated nutmeg
Salt
Freshly ground pepper
½ pound veal
½ pound pork
½ cup fresh bread crumbs from firm bread
~ 1 whole egg
Milk
12 large white mushroom caps, sliced thin
4 tablespoons flour
~ 2 egg yolks
Juice of ½ lemon
Minced parsley

Melt 4 tablespoons of the butter in a large heavy deep skillet. Add the pieces of veal (make sure the meat is dry), and sauté over moderate heat until brown all over. Add ½ cup of the broth, the thyme, bay leaf, shallots, nutmeg, and salt and pepper to taste. Cover with water, bring to a boil, cover, and simmer over low heat for 1 to 1½ hours, or until meat is tender when pierced with the point of a sharp knife. Skim off all scum as it rises to the surface.

Meanwhile, put the ½ pounds each of veal and pork through the meat grinder twice. Combine the ground meat with the bread crumbs, whole egg, and just enough milk to bind the mixture together. Shape into very tiny balls, about the size of a small walnut. Melt 4 tablespoons butter in another pan. Add the meat balls and sliced mushrooms, and sauté until meat balls have taken on color. Add meat balls and mushrooms to the stew, bring to a boil, then reduce heat to simmer.

Melt 4 tablespoons butter in another saucepan and stir in the flour until smooth. Add remaining broth and whisk briskly with a wire whip until slightly thickened. Stir into the meat mixture and simmer for 15 minutes.

Beat the egg yolks slightly, spoon a little of the hot liquid into the bowl, then stir all into the stew. Heat, but do not bring to a boil or the sauce will curdle. Take off the heat and add the lemon juice.

Spoon into a handsome tureen, already warmed, sprinkle with minced parsley, and serve with steamed rice. Serves 4 to 6.

NOTE: For a recipe for the more familiar veal blanquette which uses only egg yolks, see page 71.

Eggs and Their Other Halves in ⌇ ⌇ ⌇

Desserts

TRIFLE

Trifle is also known as Tipsy Cake, Tipsy Parson, Tipsy Squire, and even Gypsy Cake. Most modern recipes call for a spongecake base, but it's our opinion that it is best made with a rich butter cake such as poundcake. Our conviction is that the trifle originated when some thrifty English cook used up a stale piece of cake, turning it into this staggeringly rich dessert.

> Poundcake (next page), for which you need
> 9 whole eggs
> Strawberry or raspberry jam
> Cognac or brandy
> Sherry
> Crème Anglaise, half the recipe (page 110), for which you need 4 extra egg yolks
> Heavy cream
> Slivered toasted blanched almonds

Cut the cake into fingers or squares. Spread all sides of each piece with one of the jams, then pile into a handsome serving bowl. Pour 1 cup (half-and-half) Cognac or brandy and sherry over the cake. Then add the hot crème Anglaise. Refrigerate until cold.

To serve, cover thickly with whipped cream, piled high, and scatter almond slivers over the top. Serves 6.

POUNDCAKE

> 3 cups sifted all-purpose flour
> Pinch of salt
> 1 teaspoon baking powder
> 1 pound butter
> 2 cups sugar
> ~ 9 whole eggs, separated
> ½ teaspoon almond extract
> ½ teaspoon lemon extract
> ½ teaspoon rosewater

Prepare a 10-inch tube pan, coating it lightly with flour, incuding the tube (page 203). Sift the flour, salt and baking powder together twice and set aside.

Cream or work the butter with an electric mixer or with your hands until it is light and fluffy. Gradually work in the sugar until the mixture is very creamy. Beat the yolks very hard with a rotary beater or, better, an electric beater, until very thick, pale, and fluffy. Stir in the flavorings. Stir the beaten yolks into the butter-sugar mixture. Add the flour mixture, a few tablespoons at a time, stirring only until the batter is smooth. Beat the egg whites until stiff but not dry (page 201). Whip about one third of the whites into the batter with a wire whip, then fold in the remaining whites gently but thoroughly with a rubber spatula.

Pour the batter into the prepared pan and bake in a preheated 350° F. oven for 35 minutes. Reduce oven heat to 325° F. and continue baking for 25 minutes longer, or until a food pick inserted in the center comes out dry without any batter clinging to it.

To bake in loaf pans: Prepare 2 loaf pans in the same way as the tube pan, then divide the batter evenly between them. Bake in a preheated 325° F. oven (the same temperature all the way through) for 45 to 50 minutes, or until a food pick inserted in the center comes out dry and the cakes begin to shrink slightly from the sides of the pan.

Poundcake keeps well if stored in a tin securely covered, or wrapped thoroughly in foil or Saran. It freezes, of course.

LEMON SOUFFLÉ CAKE

∾ 7 whole eggs, separated
∾ 3 extra egg whites
¼ teaspoon salt
1 teaspoon cream of tartar
1½ cups superfine sugar
Grated rind of 1 lemon
1 tablespoon vanilla extract
1 cup sifted all-purpose flour
Boiled Frosting (page 164), for which
∾   you need 4 extra egg whites
Toasted shredded almonds

Place the 10 egg whites in a very large bowl, sprinkle with the salt, then beat with an electric or rotary beater until fluffy. Add the cream of tartar and continue beating until whites are stiff but not dry (page 201). Next, beat in the sugar, a small amount at a time, beating steadily until all the sugar is incorporated and the meringue is stiff and shiny.

Beat the egg yolks until very thick and creamy. Whip a few tablespoons of the meringue into the yolks with a wire whip to lighten them, then fold in the remainder thoroughly but gently. Stir in the lemon rind and vanilla. Finally, fold in the sifted flour with care.

Pour into an angel-cake pan and bake in a preheated 325° F. oven for 1 hour, or until the cake springs back when touched lightly with the tip of your finger and the cake begins to shrink ever so little from the sides of the pan. Cool in the pan.

When cold, place on a serving plate, then frost with the boiled frosting flavored with Maraschino. Frost the sides and top of the cake, then scatter toasted shredded almonds over the top.

To cut this sponge-type cake, it is best to use a serrated knife.

PÂTE À CHOUX

> 1 cup water
> ¼ pound sweet butter
> Pinch of salt
> 1 cup sifted all-purpose flour
> ∽ 4 whole eggs
> Crème Pâtissière (next page), for which
> ∽ you need 4 extra egg yolks

Combine the water, butter and salt in a heavy saucepan. Bring to a boil, take off the heat, and stir in the flour all at once. Place back over very low heat and beat vigorously with a wooden spoon until dough leaves the sides of the pan and forms a ball. Take off the heat and beat in the eggs, one at a time, beating briskly after each addition until dough is smooth. Makes 16 to 18 puffs or éclairs.

To make Cream Puffs: Drop by rounded tablespoons onto a greased baking sheet, leaving about 2 inches between puffs to allow for spreading.

To make Éclairs: Place some of the dough in a pastry bag fitted with a tube. Force through the tube onto a greased baking sheet into finger shapes about 4 inches long and 2 inches wide. Leave space to allow for spreading.

Bake either cream puffs or éclairs in a preheated 375° F. oven for 30 minutes. You can determine when they are cooked because no bubbles of fat will remain on the surface and the sides will feel rigid. Cool before using.

To fill Cream Puffs: Fill a pastry bag, fitted with a small plain tube, with crème pâtissière. Make a small opening in the bottom of each puff with a paring knife. Insert the tube into the opening and fill the puff.

To fill Éclairs: Slit each one down the side. Force crème pâtissière through a tube into the center. Finish top with Chocolate Glaze (see Glossary).

To make Beignets Soufflés: Flavor cream-puff mixture with ¼ teaspoon orange extract or 1 tablespoon dark rum. Drop by tablespoons into deep hot fat (370° F. on a thermometer). Fry until golden all over. Serve piping hot, sprinkled with confectioners' sugar.

CRÈME PÂTISSIÈRE

2 cups milk
4 egg yolks
¾ cup sugar
1 teaspoon vanilla extract
¼ cup flour

Bring the milk to a boil over moderate heat. Set aside. Combine the yolks, sugar and vanilla in a bowl and beat with a wire whip or with an electric beater until the mixture "makes ribbons" (page 39) and turns a pale yellow, 3 or 4 minutes. Add the flour and beat until smooth. Add the hot milk slowly, whipping constantly. Pour the mixture back into the saucepan, place over moderate heat, and bring to a boil, stirring constantly with a wooden spatula. Allow to boil slowly for 5 or 6 minutes, stirring all the while. Strain through a very fine sieve or several layers of cheesecloth. So a skin won't form on top, place a piece of Saran right on top of the crème. Refrigerate. Makes about 3 cups.

NOTE: Crème pâtissière is a basic cream that is used as a filling for éclairs, cream puffs, cakes, or as a base for sweet soufflés.

It can be perfumed with liqueurs such as Cognac or kirsch or with other flavors, such as coffee or almond. If you use a liqueur, add it when the cream is cold.

ZUPPA INGLESE

This is not, as the name would indicate, English soup at all, but rather a superb Italian dessert.

> Spongecake (next page), for which you need
> ∽ 4 whole eggs
> Crème Pâtissière (preceding recipe), for
> ∽ which you need 4 extra egg yolks
> ½ cup light rum
> ½ teaspoon vanilla extract
> 2 tablespoons crème de cacao
> 1 cup heavy cream, whipped
> 2 tablespoons finely chopped candied fruits

Make the spongecake. Make the crème pâtissière without the vanilla or any other flavoring. When cool, divide into 3 parts. Perfume one part with 1 tablespoon of the rum, another part with the vanilla, and the third part with the crème de cacao.

Split the 2 layers of spongecake to make 4 layers. Place one on a serving plate. Sprinkle with about 2 tablespoons of the rum and spread with one of the perfumed crèmes. Repeat with the second and third layers. Cover with the fourth layer. Sprinkle the remaining rum on top. Refrigerate over night.

Before serving, spread the whipped cream around the sides and over the top of the *zuppa* and scatter the candied fruits over all. Serves 8.

SPONGECAKE

4 whole eggs, separated
1 cup sugar
Dash of salt
½ cup potato flour*
1 teaspoon baking powder
1 teaspoon grated lemon rind

Beat the egg yolks until very thick and creamy, then beat in the sugar gradually; beat the egg whites with the salt with an electric or rotary beater until stiff but not dry (page 201).

Fold the whites into the yolk mixture thoroughly but with a gentle hand. Combine the potato flour and baking powder in a sifter and sift a small amount at a time over the egg mixture, folding in each addition carefully with a spatula. Finally, stir in the lemon rind. Pour into two 8-inch round cake pans. Place in the center of a preheated 350° F. oven and bake for 18 to 20 minutes, or until a food pick plunged in the center of the cakes comes out dry, or until the cakes spring back when touched lightly with the tip of your finger. Cool. When cold, turn out on a cake rack.

This cake can also be baked in one pan; in this case we recommend an 8-inch springform pan and baking time should be about 30 minutes. Test as you would the layers.

* This is also known as potato starch. It is available in kosher delicatessens and in Scandinavian markets, if not in your own market.

SPONGE ROLL

∾ 4 whole eggs, at room temperature
¾ teaspoon baking powder
1 teaspoon salt
¾ cup granulated sugar
½ teaspoon almond extract
¾ cup sifted cake flour
Confectioners' sugar, sifted
Crème au Beurre (next page), for which
∾ you need 5 egg yolks; or Crème Pâtissière
∾ (page 187, 4 yolks); or Rum Cream
∾ Filling (page 198, 4 yolks)

Grease a jelly-roll pan (15 x 10 inches) well and line with wax paper. Then grease the top of the paper.

Beat the whole eggs, baking powder and salt with a rotary or or electric beater until they become very thick, creamy, and light in color. Gradually beat in the granulated sugar and continue beating until the mixture "makes ribbons" (page 39) when you lift up the beater. Stir in the almond extract and beat just long enough so flavoring is well mixed into the batter. Now, fold the flour, a small amount at a time, into the batter with a rubber spatula, gently but very thoroughly.

Pour the batter into the prepared pan and smooth with a spatula so that the bottom of the pan is evenly covered. Place in a preheated 400° F. oven and bake for 13 minutes, or until cake just begins to shrink from the sides of the pan.

To make the roll: Lay a clean towel on a flat surface and sprinkle generously with confectioners' sugar. Turn the baked cake out onto the sugared towel. Lift off the wax paper immediately. Then, starting with the long side, roll up the cake and the towel, jelly-roll style; the towel will be inside the cake. Cool on a cake rack.

When the cake has cooled, unroll. Spread evenly with the

cream filling you are using. Reroll the cake carefully, sprinkle with sifted confectioners' sugar, and refrigerate until ready to serve. Bring out of the refrigerator about 30 minutes before dessert time. Serves 8 or 10.

CRÈME AU BEURRE
(*Buttercream*)

⅝ pound (2½ sticks) butter, at room
   temperature
1 cup sugar
⅓ cup water
5 egg yolks
Flavoring: 2½ tablespoons powdered instant
   coffee or ½ cup concentrated liquid coffee;
   or 3 squares (1-ounce size) unsweetened
   chocolate, melted; or ⅓ cup Grand
   Marnier or Cognac

Place the butter in a bowl and beat thoroughly with an electric beater until soft and creamy, or work well with your hands. Set aside.

To make the syrup, combine the sugar and water in a saucepan. Stir over moderate heat until the sugar has dissolved and the mixture comes to a boil. Boil very fast, without stirring, for 4 minutes.

Beat the egg yolks with the coffee or chocolate flavoring for 1 minute; if a liqueur is used, it is added later. Beat in the syrup gradually but constantly with a wire whip. When all the syrup has been incorporated, pour the mixture into the top of a double boiler and cook over simmering water, whipping constantly, for 4 or 5 minutes. At this point the mixture should be pale yellow and fluffy, with the consistency of thick cream, and should have about doubled in volume.

Take off the heat, set the pan in cold water, and whip vigorously until cream has reached room temperature. During this cooling process, the cream will thicken and get pasty. If a liqueur flavoring is used, it is beaten in at this point. Now begin to whip in the beaten butter, a small amount at a time, whipping constantly until cream is smooth and all the butter has been added. Frost cake or cakes immediately. Makes 2½ cups or enough to frost a 2-layer 8-inch cake.

∽ NOTE: If, as you add the butter, the cream stiffens too much or looks separated, it is probably because the butter is too cold. (The butter and the cream should be at the same temperature when combined.) In this case, set the bottom of the bowl in hot water for 6 to 8 seconds and stir very well with a wooden or rubber spatula. If it should be necessary to refrigerate the crème au beurre before using, soften in the same way, by stirring over hot water.

DÉLICE DE BELGIQUE
(Rum Chocolate Cream)

> 2 cups heavy cream
> 2 cups milk
> ½ cup sugar
> 1 tablespoon cornstarch
> ∽ 6 egg yolks, well beaten
> ½ cup dark rum
> 5 tablespoons cold water
> Ladyfingers (page 193), for which you need
> ∽ 2 whole eggs and 1 extra egg white
> ∽ 3 egg whites
> ½ ounce unsweetened chocolate, grated

Combine the heavy cream, 1½ cups of the milk and the sugar in the top of a double boiler. Stir constantly, over low heat, until the sugar has dissolved. Bring to a boil, then take off the heat immediately.

Meanwhile, mix the cornstarch with the remaining milk until smooth. Stir into the well-beaten yolks thoroughly. Add a few tablespoons of the hot milk mixture to the yolk mixture, then combine the two. Place over simmering water (make sure the bottom of the pan does not touch the water) and cook, whipping constantly, until the custard has thickened and coats a spoon. Take off the heat and refrigerate. To prevent a skin forming, lay a piece of Saran right on top of the custard.

When cold, stir in 3 tablespoons of the rum. Combine the remaining rum with the cold water. Sprinkle both sides of the ladyfingers with the rum-and-water mixture and use them to line the bottom and sides of a 1½-quart serving bowl or charlotte mold.

Beat the egg whites until stiff but not dry (page 201). Beat about one third of the whites into the custard with a whip thoroughly, then fold in remainder with care. Spoon into the lady-finger-lined bowl, sprinkle the top with grated chocolate, and refrigerate for several hours. Serves 6.

LADYFINGERS

⅓ cup sifted all-purpose flour
Good pinch of salt
2 whole eggs, separated
1 extra egg white
⅓ cup sifted confectioners' sugar
½ teaspoon vanilla extract
Confectioners' sugar, sifted

Sift the flour with the salt two or three times and set aside; grease 2 baking sheets lightly, then coat with flour, dumping off any excess; beat the yolks with an electric or rotary beater until very thick and pale. Set aside.

Beat the whites until stiff but not dry (page 201). Then

gradually beat in the sugar until you have a thick shiny meringue. Beat the yolks with the vanilla thoroughly, then fold into the meringue. Add flour to the mixture in one fell swoop, blending only long enough to incorporate it. The batter should remain light but firm. Scoop some of the batter into a pastry bag and squeeze out the "fingers," approximately 4 inches long and 1½ inches wide, a good inch apart. Continue until all the batter has been used. Sprinkle the fingers with sifted confectioners' sugar.

Place on the middle and upper racks of a preheated 300° F. oven and bake for 20 minutes; the "fingers" should be pale beige with a slight crust when cooked properly. Once they are taken from the oven, remove immediately from baking sheets and cool on cake racks. Makes about 12 to 14.

Ladyfingers are served plain with tea or with fruit or frozen desserts. They are sometimes put together in pairs with a coating of Apricot Glaze (see Glossary) between, or a thin coating of whipped cream. And, of course, they are used as an ingredient in innumerable dessert recipes.

BAVAROIS BRESSAN

> 3 cups Crème Anglaise (page 110), for
> ~ which you need 6 egg yolks
> 2 envelopes unflavored gelatin
> 3 squares (1-ounce size) semisweet chocolate or
> 3 ounces semisweet chocolate pieces
> ⅜ pound sweet butter (1½ sticks), softened
> ½ teaspoon almond extract
> 4 ounces blanched almonds, finely grated
> Ladyfingers (page 193), for which you need
> ~ 2 whole eggs and 1 extra egg white
> Dark rum, kirsch, Cognac or Grand Marnier
> 1½ cups Crème Chantilly (see Glossary)
> Candied violets (optional)

To make 3 cups of crème Anglaise, use only 6 egg yolks and reduce all other proportions by one fourth. In the initial step, combine the gelatin with the yolks, sugar, etc., then continue to follow
the directions.

Measure 1 cup of the hot crème Anglaise into a saucepan, add
the chocolate, and heat, stirring constantly, until chocolate softens.
Take off the heat and stir vigorously until chocolate is thoroughly
mixed in. Set aside to cool. Cool the remainder of the crème to
room temperature.

When the chocolate mixture is cool, whip with an electric or
rotary beater until fluffy, then beat in the softened butter and the
almond extract until well incorporated. Then, mix in the grated
almonds. Stir in the remaining cooled crème, and refrigerate until
it is just barely beginning to set. This takes a very short time.

Meanwhile, line a 1-quart mold with ladyfingers, crust side
against the mold. Sprinkle a tablespoon or so of one of the liqueurs
over them. Spoon the cream into the prepared mold carefully so as
not to disturb the "fingers," and refrigerate until firm.

To serve, turn the Bavarois out on a cold serving platter and
cover with crème Chantilly pushed through a pastry tube. Decorate with candied violets. Serves 8.

LEMON MERINGUE PIE

Lemon Butter (page 196), for which you
need 3 whole eggs and 1 extra egg yolk
1 baked 8-inch pastry shell
2 egg whites
½ cup sugar

Spoon the cooled Lemon Butter into the pastry shell and smooth
with a spatula.

Beat the egg whites until stiff but not dry (page 201), then begin to add the sugar, 1 tablespoon or so at a time, beating constantly and vigorously until all the sugar is incorporated. Spoon over the top of the filling, spreading the meringue so it touches the pastry all around.

Place the pie on the center rack of a preheated 350° F. oven and bake until the meringue is flecked with gold. Cool but do not refrigerate. Neither pastry nor meringue responds well to refrigeration. Serves 6.

LEMON BUTTER

This old English recipe is also known as lemon curd and lemon cheese. It is used to fill tarts, pies, cakes and, in England, is served on toast or biscuits at teatime. Refrigerated in a tightly covered jar, lemon butter will keep for weeks.

> ∽ 3 whole eggs
> ∽ 1 extra egg yolk
> 1 cup sugar
> Juice of 1 lemon
> ¼ pound sweet butter
> Grated rind of 2 lemons

Combine the whole eggs, extra yolk, sugar, lemon juice, and butter in the top of a double boiler. Mix together very well, then place over simmering water (over, not in) and cook, stirring constantly, until mixture is as thick as heavy mayonnaise. This will take from 25 to 30 minutes. Take off the heat and cool. When cool, stir in the grated lemon rind. This amount of lemon butter will fill one 8-inch pie shell, 6 tart shells, or a 3-layer cake.

To make Lime Butter: Use the juice from 3 limes and the grated rind of 2 limes in place of the lemon. All other ingredients remain the same, as do the cooking instructions.

CREAM PIE

>   1¾ cups sifted all-purpose flour
>   2 teaspoons baking powder
>   ¼ teaspoon salt
>   5½ tablespoons (a little over ½ stick) butter
>   1 cup granulated sugar
>   2 whole eggs, separated
>   1 teaspoon vanilla extract
>   ½ cup milk
>   ½ recipe Crème au Beurre (page 191, for
>   which you need 2½ egg yolks); or Crème
>   Pâtissière (page 187, 2 yolks); or Rum
>   Cream Filling (page 198, 2 yolks)
>   Confectioners' sugar, sifted

Prepare two 8-inch cake pans, coating them with flour (page 203). Sift the flour with the baking powder and salt. Set aside.

Cream the butter with an electric beater or by hand until soft and light. Work in the sugar gradually and continue creaming until mixture is very fluffy. Add the yolks, one at a time, beating vigorously after each addition. Add the vanilla. Stir in the sifted flour and the milk alternately, with a spatula, beginning and ending with flour.

Beat the egg whites until stiff but not dry (page 201). Then fold into the batter with a spatula gently but thoroughly. Divide the batter evenly between the two prepared pans. Place the pans on the middle rack in a preheated 375° F. oven and bake for 20 to 25 minutes, or until a toothpick inserted in the center comes out dry. Turn out of pans at once and cool on a cake rack.

Spread the cream filling you are using between the cooled layers and sprinkle the top with sifted confectioners' sugar. Serves 6 to 8.

RUM CREAM FILLING

> 2 cups Crème Pâtissière (page 187), for
> which you need 4 egg yolks
> ½ cup dark rum*
> ¼ pound sweet butter, softened

If the crème pâtissière has been refrigerated, bring to room temperature. Stir in the rum, then beat in the softened butter with a wire whip, bit by bit, until all is incorporated. This makes a delicious filling for éclairs and cream puffs; it can also be used to frost cakes, and it is an excellent substitute for Crème au Beurre (page 191) which is somewhat more complicated to make.

* Other suitable flavorings are Grand Marnier, Cognac and kirsch. If the latter, use only ⅓ cup rather than ½ cup. *Note well, the liqueur should be added before the butter.*

CLASSIC GÉNOISE

> 6 whole eggs
> 1¼ cups sugar, in all
> ¾ cup sifted all-purpose flour
> ¼ cup water
> Crème au Beurre (page 191, for which you
> need 5 egg yolks); or Crème Pâtissière
> (page 187, 4 yolks); or Rum Cream
> Filling (page 198, 4 yolks)

Prepare a 9-inch round cake pan, coating it with flour (page 203). Set aside.

Place the eggs and ¾ cup of the sugar in the top of a double boiler, over warm, not hot, water and beat with a rotary or electric beater until the mixture "makes ribbons" (page 39). This calls for steady, vigorous, unremitting beating. The secret in making this famous French cake successfully is temperature. The mixture should never be allowed to get hot but is, rather, kept tepid throughout this beating period.

Take off the heat and out of the double boiler, and continue beating until mixture reaches room temperature. At this point, sift the flour over the mixture a small quantity at a time, folding it in after each addition, thoroughly but gently. Pour the batter into the prepared pan.

Bake in a preheated 400° F. oven for 30 to 35 minutes, or until a toothpick inserted in the center comes out dry. Turn out of the pan immediately onto a cake rack to cool. When cold, split in two horizontally.

While the cake is baking, make up this "simple syrup": Combine the remaining ½ cup sugar with the ¼ cup water. Stir over moderate heat until dissolved, then bring to a boil without stirring. Cook for a few minutes, until syrup has thickened slightly. Perfume with dark rum or kirsch, or whatever flavoring is used in the filling. Spoon the syrup over the cut sides of the génoise. Fill and frost with whichever cream you are using.

Eggs and Their Other Halves in ∾ ∾ ∾

Soufflés

Of all the great works of French architecture—Notre-Dame, Mont St. Michel, Chambord, the Eiffel Tower—the soufflé is the only one whose foundation is flour, butter, a liquid and eggs. The word comes from *souffler,* to breathe, inflate, puff up, and there's no reason on earth why this lovely noun has to take the verb "fall." The old wive's tale that one cross word in the kitchen makes the soufflé tumble just isn't true. Properly made, a good soufflé should be able to withstand snow, rain, heat, gloom of night and the clump of the courtier's boot. The only caveat is timing. A soufflé must, must, *must* go direct from oven to table. Like all things capricious, elegant and desirable, the dish cannot be kept waiting. Even if your guests haven't quite finished their drinks, make them come straight to the dining room.

The soufflé is nothing more than a thick sauce into which egg yolks, butter, a flavoring and, finally, beaten egg whites are incorporated. It is the air, beaten into the egg whites in the form of little bubbles, which expands as the soufflé is cooked, that pushes it up into its magnificent puff. The flavoring element can be almost anything—cheese, chocolate, lemon, orange, chicken, corn, oysters, even peanut butter, if you go in for that kind of thing. It is an accommodating dish. A cheese soufflé makes a splendid first course. One made from fowl or fish is a meal in itself. One with a sweet flavor—chocolate or any of the fruits or liqueurs—makes an incomparable dessert. The main points to remember about making and baking soufflés are these:

The Whip and the Whites. The big balloon whip (*fouet* in French) is preferred by chefs and many cooking authorities because you can keep the whole mass of egg whites in continual air-circulating motion, the whites mount faster, and you get greater volume. Nevertheless, most home cooks will continue to use the rotary or electric beater, or electric mixer, which make less rigorous demands on the cook's muscles. A damp cloth under a bowl while whipping helps to prevent it sliding and also cuts down the racket.

The small whip, which comes in varying sizes, is used in innumerable ways in the kitchen: to incorporate the first batch of whites into the soufflé base; to whip a *beurre manié* into a hot liquid; to make a Béchamel; to beat or stir any mixture that should be kept in continual motion.

Stiff but Not Dry. This is the accepted term. This means the whites are beaten to the point where they stand in glossy peaks, look "wet," and cling tightly to the whip or beater when it is held straight up. This is the correct stage for all beaten whites, for all recipes, unless the recipe specifies otherwise. If whipped to the dry stage, they become granular and will break up when folded into the main mixture. A soufflé, for example, would not rise and would be grainy in the center.

Extra Egg Whites. Most French soufflé recipes call for at least 1 extra egg white to 4 whole eggs. But chefs are inclined to add more whites, almost at will, to give extra lightness to the soufflé. There's a point beyond which you can't and should not go, but 3 extra whites is not unusual. And, if you have them on hand, why not toss them in the ring?

Folding. This means incorporating a fragile mixture, such as beaten egg whites, very delicately into a heavier mixture, such as a soufflé base or a cake batter. The objective is to retain the air already beaten into the whites. With soufflés, you beat about one third of the beaten whites into the base thoroughly, whipping vigorously with a whip. Then with a rubber spatula you scoop the remaining whites on top of the mixture. To fold: Cut the spatula down from the center to the bottom of the pan or bowl, then run it along the bottom toward you and against the edge of the pan, rotating the pan as you work. Make sure the spatula reaches to the very bottom and sides of the mixture and brings the mixture up over the top. Keep repeating the process until all the whites have been folded in. Do not attempt to fold in every last bit of the whites—a few unblended patches are par for the soufflé course.

The Soufflé Mold. Although a soufflé can be baked in any fairly shallow (approximately 3 inches high) ovenproof dish, it is more attractive to use the straight-sided French porcelain soufflé dish. These are usually available in the housewares departments of good stores and shops that carry French cooking equipment. The mold comes in three sizes: 1 quart, 1½ quarts, and 2 quarts.

The 2-quart is the largest mold for a good reason; soufflés cannot be doubled because the batter would not cook in the required length of time. If you want to serve more people than 1 recipe will accommodate, make 2 soufflés.

Some American recipes call for a collar (foil or wax paper) around the mold to give the soufflé added height. If the soufflé has been properly made, and the mold properly prepared (below), this is completely unnecessary. In the case of cold soufflés (page 111), the collar is for effect only, because these are not true soufflés and they are not baked; therefore, the crown is "faked" in this manner.

Preparing the Soufflé Mold. The bottom and sides should be buttered heavily, taking care to get the butter into the curve at the bottom of the mold. The mold is then coated with grated cheese, bread crumbs, flour or sugar (sometimes a combination of the last two), depending on the type of soufflé. To coat, spoon several tablespoons of the coating ingredient into the mold. Then, holding the mold in your hands, roll it around and around so that sides and bottom are evenly but lightly coated. Turn it upside down and give it a good bang to get rid of any surplus coating.

Soufflé Collar. Cut a piece of wax paper long enough to fit inside the top of the soufflé mold and overlap generously. Fold it so you have a double fold, then cut it to a depth of about 3 inches. Fasten the ends together with paper clips.

When the soufflé mixture is ready, pour it into the mold to the very top. Now, tuck the collar inside the mold (the soufflé mixture should hold it), leaving 2½ inches of the collar above the mold. Add the remainder of the soufflé, taking care not to disturb the paper.

Chilling the Mold. This professional chef's trick, which helps the soufflé not only to rise, but to rise straight up, is called for in our hot soufflé recipes. Refrigerate the prepared mold for 30 minutes, or longer, but no less. If time is pressing, stick it in the freezer to speed the chilling.

Oven Temperature and Placement of Mold. Preheat the oven to whatever temperature is called for in the recipe. Place the mold on the rack at the middle level of the oven, to give the most even distribution of the heat. Some authorities recommend placing the mold on a baking sheet which has been standing in the oven so that it is already hot. In this way cooking starts from the bottom as well as the top and the overly liquid layer, which sometimes remains in the bottom, is avoided.

When is the Soufflé Done? When it has risen 2 or 3 inches above the level at which it went into the oven, it is approaching doneness; certain soufflés, notably vegetable, meat, fish, and chocolate, will not rise to such dazzling heights. Broadly speaking, most soufflés will cook in 25 to 30 minutes. For those who like a creamy center, the soufflé should be baked a few minutes less than the time indicated in the recipe. About 10 minutes before the baking time is up, give the soufflé mold a gentle shove. If the top "shivers," the soufflé is still creamy inside.

Serving the Soufflé. Place a fresh white linen napkin, folded, on a tray and set the hot soufflé dish on top of the napkin. This not only makes the presentation more attractive but, more importantly, keeps the dish from sliding around when the soufflé is being served.

How Many Will a Soufflé Serve? A main-dish soufflé baked in a 1-quart mold may be only enough for 2 people if the rest of the meal is simple. A 1½-quart soufflé may serve 4 if it is a main dish, or perhaps 6 if it is a vegetable soufflé served as an accompaniment to a main dish. A 2-quart soufflé will serve

5 to 8, depending on whether it is a main dish or an accompaniment.

Dessert soufflés may make more servings if the rest of the meal has been ample and the soufflé is very rich, but on the other hand, if the soufflé is superb, it may be hard to stretch it to serve more than 4 people; perhaps only 2 or 3 will be able to eat it all.

BASIC CHEESE SOUFFLÉ

> ¾ cup freshly grated Swiss cheese, or half
>   Swiss and half Parmesan*
> 1 cup Sauce Béchamel**
> 1 thin slice Swiss cheese
> ∾ 4 whole eggs, separated
> ∾ 3 extra egg whites

Prepare a 1-quart soufflé mold, coating it with flour or cheese (page 203). Refrigerate. Cut the cheese slice into strips, squares, or diamonds. Set aside.

With a wire whisk, beat the egg yolks one at a time into the lukewarm Béchamel. (*The soufflé can be prepared to this point and set aside covered with a seal of Saran wrap.*) Beat the 7 egg whites until stiff but not dry. With the wire whip, beat about one third of the whites vigorously into the sauce. Add half the grated cheese. Then fold (page 202) in gradually the remaining whites alternately with the remaining grated cheese.

Pour the batter into the prepared mold, smooth the top with a spatula, and arrange the sliced cheese on the soufflé. Place in a pre-heated 400° F. oven, turn down the heat immediately to 375° F., and bake the soufflé for 25 to 30 minutes. For a firm rather than a creamy center, bake an additional 5 minutes. Serves 3 or 4.

---

* With American cheddar cheese, use only ⅔ cup of grated natural cheddar, because it is somewhat heavier than the other cheeses suggested. Do not use nutmeg in the Béchamel.

** Make the Sauce Béchamel (see Glossary) in these proportions: 3 tablespoons butter, 3 tablespoons flour, 1 cup milk, ½ teaspoon salt, a dash of freshly ground white pepper, and a pinch each of cayenne and nutmeg.

SOUFFLÉ LAURETTE

1 cup Sauce Béchamel*
½ cup freshly grated Parmesan cheese
6 whole eggs, separated
2 or 3 extra egg whites
6 whole eggs

Prepare a 1½quart soufflé dish, coating it with grated Parmesan cheese (page 203). Refrigerate.

Stir the ½ cup of grated cheese into the hot Béchamel and let it cool to lukewarm. With a wire whisk, beat in the 6 egg yolks, one at a time. Put the sauce back over moderate heat and cook for 2 or 3 minutes, stirring constantly. Do not allow it to come to a boil.

Beat the 8 separated egg whites until stiff but not dry (page 201). Whip about one third of the beaten whites into the cheese sauce vigorously. Then fold (page 202) in the remainder. Pour half of the mixture into the prepared mold. Break over it the whole eggs, one at a time. Spoon the remainder of the sauce mixture over the uncooked eggs. Smooth the surface with a flexible spatula.

Place in a preheated 375° F. oven and bake for 30 to 35 minutes, or until nicely puffed and golden. Serve immediately. Serves 6.

* Make the Sauce Béchamel (see Glossary) in these proportions: 4 tablespoons butter, 4 tablespoons flour, and 1 cup milk. Season with salt and freshly ground white pepper.

SOUFFLÉ DE HOMARD À L'AMÉRICAINE
(Lobster Soufflé)

The sauce Américaine not only goes into the soufflé but is served with it. So it must be made first.

Sauce Américaine

1 live lobster (2 to 2½ pounds)
4 tablespoons butter, softened
1 cup dry white wine
2 tablespoons flour
¼ cup olive oil
Salt
Freshly ground pepper
3 shallots, chopped
1 small white onion, chopped
1 garlic clove, crushed
¼ cup Cognac
2 cups fish stock or clam juice
2 fresh tomatoes, coarsely chopped
10 leaves of fresh tarragon, chopped, or
   1 teaspoon dried tarragon
Few parsley sprigs
Good dash of cayenne pepper

Have the fishmonger cut the lobster, if you're not up to it yourself, in this fashion: Sever the claws; cut the tail sections; split the body into halves lengthwise; remove and discard the little bag near the head. An effort should be made to save as much as possible of the liquid that comes from the lobster, and, of course, the tomalley (liver) and the coral if it happens to be a hen lobster.

Combine all the juices, tomalley and coral with half of the softened butter, half of the wine and the 2 tablespoons of flour. Mix thoroughly to make a smooth purée and set aside.

Heat the olive oil and remaining butter in a large heavy skillet until very hot. Season the lobster pieces with salt and pepper, and sauté in the hot oil and butter for several minutes, turning occasionally, until the shells turn bright red. Add the shallots, onion and garlic. Place the skillet over moderate heat, add the Cognac and ignite. Shake the pan until the flames die out. Add all remaining ingredients, cover tightly, and simmer for 20 to 25 minutes.

Lift the lobster pieces out of the cooking liquid. Take the meat out of the shells, discard shells, and set the meat aside. Stir the reserved tomalley purée into the mixture in the pan and cook slowly for 15 to 20 minutes. Then press the sauce through a very fine sieve. Set aside one third of the sauce to serve with the soufflé and combine the remainder with the lobster meat. Keep warm. All this can be done ahead of time.

The Soufflé:

~ 4 whole eggs, separated
1 cup Sauce Béchamel*
~ 2 or 3 extra egg whites
2 tablespoons grated Gruyère cheese
Sauce Américaine (above)
½ cup heavy cream
1 jigger (3 tablespoons) Cognac

Prepare a 1-quart soufflé mold, coating it with flour (page 203). Refrigerate.

With a wire whisk, beat the 4 yolks one at a time into the lukewarm Béchamel. (*The soufflé can be prepared to this point and set aside, sealed with Saran wrap.*) Beat the egg whites until stiff but not dry (page 201). Then whip about one third into the sauce Béchamel, with the cheese, briskly and thoroughly. Fold (page 202) in the remainder.

* Make the Sauce Béchamel (see Glossary) in these proportions: 2 tablespoons butter, 2 tablespoons flour and 1 cup milk.

Pour lobster and sauce Américaine mixture into the prepared mold (this should half fill the mold). Pour the soufflé mixture on top and smooth the surface with a spatula. Score the surface of the soufflé lightly with the point of a sharp knife.

Bake in a preheated 375° F. oven for 25 to 30 minutes. While the soufflé is baking, bring the reserved sauce Américaine to a boil, then stir in the cream and the Cognac. Serve on the side in a warm sauceboat. Serves 4.

SOUFFLE AUX FRUITS DE MER

½ pound poached sole fillets
¾ cup Sauce Béchamel*
¼ pound cooked sea scallops, cut into small dice
¼ pound cooked lobster meat,
    cut into small dice
3 or 4 fresh mushrooms, sautéed,
    cut into small dice
Salt
Freshly ground white pepper
~ 4 whole eggs, separated
~ 2 or 3 extra egg whites

Prepare a 1-quart soufflé dish, coating it with flour (page 203). Refrigerate.

Purée the cooked sole in the electric blender or push through a very fine sieve. Mix into the hot sauce Béchamel thoroughly, then stir in the scallops, lobster meat and the mushrooms. Bring to a boil over moderate heat. Take off the heat and add seasoning to

---

* Make the Sauce Béchamel (see Glossary) in these proportions: 3 tablespoons butter, 3 tablespoons flour, and 1 cup milk, seasoned with salt and freshly ground white pepper.

taste. Cool slightly. With a wire whisk, beat the 4 yolks one at a time into the fish mixture. (*The soufflé can be prepared to this point and set aside. If set aside, seal with Saran wrap.*)

Beat the egg whites until stiff but not dry (page 201). Whip about one third into the soufflé base vigorously with a wire whip. Fold (page 202) in the remainder. Pour into the prepared mold and bake in a preheated 400° F. oven for 25 minutes. Serve with Lobster Sauce (page 177). Serves 4.

OYSTER SOUFFLÉ

> 18 oysters in their liquor
> Freshly grated Parmesan cheese (about ½ cup)
> Olive oil (about ⅓ cup)
> 1 small garlic clove, minced
> Cracker crumbs (about 1 cup)
> Freshly ground white pepper
> 6 eggs, separated
> 1 cup Sauce Béchamel*
> 3 extra egg whites

Prepare a 1½-quart soufflé mold, coating it with grated Parmesan cheese (page 203). Refrigerate.

Drain the liquor from the oysters into a measuring cup. Purée 6 of the oysters in an electric blender, then combine with the oyster liquor. You should have 1 cup altogether. If not, add enough milk to make a full cup. Set aside to use for the liquid in the sauce Béchamel.

Place about ½ cup of grated cheese in a bowl. Put the olive oil

* Make the Sauce Béchamel (see Glossary) in these proportions: 4 tablespoons butter, 4 tablespoons flour, the cup of oyster liquor (in place of milk) and salt and freshly ground white pepper to taste.

well mixed with the garlic in a second bowl. Put the cracker crumbs well seasoned with pepper in a third bowl. Dry the remaining oysters very well with paper towels. Dip each oyster first into the cheese; then into the oil mixture; then roll in the cracker crumbs. Place on a tray and set aside.

With a wire whisk, beat the 6 yolks one at a time into the lukewarm sauce Béchamel. (*The soufflé can be prepared to this point and set aside, sealed with Saran wrap.*)

Beat the 9 egg whites until stiff but not dry (page 201). Whip about one third of the beaten whites into the sauce vigorously with a wire whip. Fold (page 202) in the remainder.

Pour half of the soufflé mixture into the prepared mold. Arrange oysters on top, cover with the remainder of the mixture, and sprinkle the top with grated cheese. Bake in a preheated 375° F. oven for 30 to 35 minutes. Serves 5 to 6.

Serve as a main course at lunch, or as an accompaniment to thinly sliced cold smoked ham.

CAULIFLOWER SOUFFLÉ

1 small cauliflower (about 4 inches in
    diameter)
1½ cups milk
1½ cups water
Salt
½ cup Sauce Béchamel*
6 tablespoons freshly grated
    Parmesan cheese (about)
½ teaspoon lemon juice
1 teaspoon grated onion
Freshly ground white pepper
3 whole eggs, separated
2 or 3 extra egg whites
1 tablespoon melted butter

Prepare a 1-quart soufflé dish (page 203), coating it with grated
Parmesan cheese. Refrigerate.

Peel the leaves off the cauliflower and cut off the base, but
leave the head whole. Combine the milk and water with 1 teaspoon
salt. Add the cauliflower, bring to a boil, and cook over moderate
heat until tender but still shapely. Drain upside down thoroughly.

To the hot sauce Bèchamel add half of the Parmesan cheese
and the lemon juice, grated onion, a dash of salt, and several
grinds of the peppermill. Simmer, stirring constantly, for a few
minutes. With a wire whisk, beat the 3 egg yolks one at a time into
the lukewarm sauce Béchamel. Cool slightly. (*The soufflé can
be prepared to this point and set aside, with a seal of Saran wrap.*)

Beat the whites until stiff but not dry (page 201), then whip
about one third into the sauce mixture with a wire whip, en-
thusiastically. Fold (page 202) remainder in gently. Place the

---

* Make the Sauce Béchamel (see Glossary) in these proportions:
2 tablespoons butter, 2 tablespoons flour, and ½ cup milk.

cooked cauliflower in the prepared soufflé mold, cover with the sauce, and sprinkle with the remaining cheese and the melted butter.

Bake in a preheated 350° F. oven for 25 minutes. Serve with Sauce Hollandaise (page 87) as a main course, or serve as an accompaniment to cold ham, corned beef or smoked tongue. Serves 4.

MUSHROOM SOUFFLÉ

2 tablespoons butter
½ pound fresh mushrooms, minced
4 whole eggs, separated
1 cup Sauce Béchamel*
2 or 3 extra egg whites

Butter a 1-quart soufflé dish, coating it with bread crumbs (page 203). Refrigerate.

Melt the butter in a saucepan, add the mushrooms, and sauté for about 3 minutes without allowing them to take on color. Purée in the electric blender or pass through a food mill.

With a wire whisk, beat the 4 egg yolks one at a time into the lukewarm Béchamel. (*The soufflé can be prepared to this point and set aside, sealed with Saran wrap.*)

Whip the egg whites until stiff but not dry (page 201). Then whip about a third into the mixture vigorously. Fold in the mushroom purée, then fold in the remaining whites.

Pour into the prepared soufflé dish, place in a preheated 375° F. oven, and bake for 30 to 35 minutes. Serves 4 to 6.

* Make the Sauce Béchamel (see Glossary) in these proportions: 3 tablespoons butter, 3 tablespoons flour, 1 cup milk, seasoned with salt, freshly ground white pepper, and a good pinch of freshly grated nutmeg.

ONION SOUFFLÉ

1 large onion, chopped fine
1 cup milk
Salt
Freshly ground white pepper
4 tablespoons butter
4 tablespoons flour
5 whole eggs, separated
2 or 3 extra egg whites

Butter a 1-quart soufflé mold thoroughly, and coat with grated Parmesan cheese (page 203). Refrigerate.

Combine the chopped onion with the milk and salt and pepper to taste, and cook, over a moderate heat, until the onion is tender. Pour into the electric blender and blend until smooth. Melt the butter in a saucepan, blend in the flour and cook, over moderate heat, 3 to 4 minutes. Add the onion milk, beating constantly, and cook until the mixture is very thick. Cool slightly. With a wire whip, beat the 5 egg yolks thoroughly, one at a time into the luke-warm onion sauce. (*The soufflé can be prepared to this point and set aside, sealed with Saran wrap*).

Beat the egg whites until stiff but not dry (page 201). Whip one third of the whites into the sauce vigorously with a whisk. Then fold (page 202) in the remainder. Pour into the prepared mold, smooth the top with a spatula, and bake in a preheated 375° F. oven for 30 to 35 minutes, or until the soufflé is well puffed and lightly browned. Serve immediately. Serves 6 if served with meat or 4 as a main course.

Onion soufflé is delicious with any meat with which onion is sympatico—beef, steak, lamb, or the fowl family.

INDIVIDUAL FRESH-CORN SOUFFLÉS

> 4 tablespoons butter
> 2 tablespoons chopped onion
> 5 tablespoons flour
> 1 teaspoon salt
> Dash of freshly ground white pepper
> ¾ cup milk
> 2 cups corn scraped from the cob
>   (4 to 6 ears)
> ∾ 5 whole eggs, separated
> ∾ 2 extra egg whites

Prepare 6 individual soufflé dishes. Butter well, then coat them with either fine bread crumbs or grated Parmesan cheese (page 203). Refrigerate.

Melt the butter in a pan, add the onion and cook over moderate heat until onion is limp and transparent. Do not allow it to brown. Stir in the flour, salt and pepper and cook, stirring constantly, for 2 or 3 minutes. Add the milk and cook, stirring constantly, until sauce comes to a boil and thickens. Stir in the fresh corn and cook for 1 minute longer. Take off the heat and cool slightly. With a wire whisk, beat the 5 egg yolks thoroughly, one at a time, into the corn mixture.

Beat the 7 egg whites until stiff but not dry (page 201). Whip about one third of the whites into the sauce vigorously. Fold (page 202) in remainder. Pour into the prepared molds and bake in a 375° F. oven for 15 to 20 minutes.

SOUFFLÉ AUX PETITS POIS

1 package (10 ounces) frozen *petits pois*
1 cup Sauce Béchamel*
4 whole eggs, separated
2 or 3 extra egg whites

Prepare a 1-quart soufflé dish, coating it with fine bread crumbs (page 203). Refrigerate.

Thaw the peas, then place in the container of an electric blender and blend for a second or so, only long enough to break up some, but not all, of the peas. Combine with the hot sauce Béchamel. Cool slightly. With a wire whisk, beat the 4 egg yolks one at a time into the sauce. (*The soufflé can be prepared to this point and set aside, with a seal of Saran wrap.*)

Beat the egg whites until stiff but not dry (page 201). Whip about one third of the beaten whites into the pea mixture vigorously. Then fold (page 202) in the remainder.

Pour into the prepared mold and bake in a preheated 375° F. oven for 30 minutes, or until the soufflé has puffed noticeably and browned lightly.

Serve with any meat or fish with which peas are compatible. Serves 4.

* Make the Sauce Béchamel (see Glossary) in these proportions: 3 tablespoons butter, 3 tablespoons flour, 1 cup milk, seasoned with salt, freshly ground white pepper, and a good pinch of freshly grated nutmeg.

SQUASH SOUFFLÉ

> 2 cups cooked winter squash or 1 package
>   (12 ounces) frozen squash, thawed
> 1 cup Sauce Béchamel*
> Salt
> Freshly ground white pepper
> ∽ 4 whole eggs, separated
> ∽ 2 or 3 extra egg whites

Prepare a 1-quart soufflé mold, coating with fine bread crumbs (page 203). Refrigerate.

Stir the cooked or thawed squash, first mashed to a smooth purée, into the sauce Béchamel, and season with salt and pepper to taste. With a wire whisk, beat the 4 egg yolks one at a time into the lukewarm mixture. (*The soufflé can be prepared to this point and set aside, sealed with Saran wrap.*)

Beat the egg whites until stiff but not dry (page 201). Whip about one third of the whites into the squash mixture vigorously. Then fold (page 202) in remainder.

Pour into the prepared soufflé mold and bake in a preheated 375° F. oven for about 30 minutes, or until soufflé has puffed and browned lightly.

Serve immediately with roast or broiled chicken, turkey, roast beef or steak. Serves 4.

---

*Make the Sauce Béchamel (see Glossary) in these proportions: 3 tablespoons butter, 3 tablespoons flour, 1 cup milk, seasoned with salt and freshly ground white pepper.

FRESH-TOMATO SOUFFLÉ

> 6 medium-sized ripe fresh tomatoes
> 1 small yellow onion, chopped
> 1 large garlic clove, mashed
> ½ teaspoon sugar
> ¼ teaspoon dried basil
> 1 teaspoon salt
> Freshly ground pepper
> 3 tablespoons butter
> 4 tablespoons flour
> 6 whole eggs, separated
> 2 or 3 extra egg whites
> Freshly grated Parmesan cheese

Prepare a 1½-quart soufflé dish, coating it with grated Parmesan cheese (page 203). Refrigerate.

Peel, seed and dice the tomatoes (see Glossary). Combine in a heavy saucepan with the onion, garlic, sugar, basil, salt and a few twists from the peppermill. Bring to a boil over high heat, then cook over moderate heat until sauce has reduced to 1¾ cups. Purée in an electric blender, or rub mixture through a very fine sieve.

Melt the butter in a heavy pan, stir in flour until smooth, and cook until butter froths. Take off the heat and stir in the tomato purée. With a wire whisk, beat the 6 egg yolks one at a time into the lukewarm tomato sauce. (*The soufflé can be prepared to this point and set aside, sealed with Saran wrap.*)

Beat the egg whites until stiff but not dry (page 201), then whip about one third into the tomato mixture vigorously with a wire whip. Fold (page 202) in the remainder.

Pour into the prepared mold, smooth the surface, and sprinkle with the Parmesan cheese. Bake in a preheated 375° F. oven for 30 to 35 minutes. Serves 6.

POTATO SOUFFLÉ WITH GARLIC

2 heads garlic, about 30 cloves
4 tablespoons butter
2 tablespoons flour
1 cup milk, heated
¼ teaspoon salt
Pinch white pepper
2 pounds baking potatoes (about 3),
   peeled and quartered
∾ 4 whole eggs
∾ 2 or 3 extra egg whites

Prepare a 1-quart soufflé dish (page 203), coating it with grated Parmesan. Refrigerate.

Separate the garlic cloves, drop into boiling water, and boil for 2 minutes. Drain and peel. Melt the butter in a heavy saucepan, then cook the garlic in it slowly, covered, for about 20 minutes, or until tender but not browned. Blend in the flour and cook, over a low heat, until the mixture froths. Cook for 2 minutes without browning. Off heat, stir in the milk, salt and pepper. Purée in the electric blender or push through a sieve. Return to the fire and simmer for 2 more minutes. Set aside.

Drop the potatoes into enough boiling salted water to cover, and boil until tender when pierced with a small pointed knife. Drain immediately and dry over a high flame, then put through a potato ricer. Give the potatoes a good beating over a moderate heat to rid them of any moisture. Heat the garlic sauce to the boiling point, then beat into the hot potatoes vigorously. Cool slightly.

With a wire whisk, beat the 4 yolks one at a time into the lukewarm potato mixture. Whip the whites until they stand in peaks when you hold up the beater. Whip about a third into the potatoes, then fold in the remainder. Pour into the prepared soufflé dish, and bake in a preheated 375° F. oven for 45 minutes. Serve with broiled or baked fish, shad roe, or lamb, veal or chicken. Serves 6.

SOUFFLÉ DI RISO
(*Rice Soufflé*)

> 2 cups grated Swiss cheese
> ¾ cup rice
> 2 cups milk
> 2 cups Sauce Béchamel*
> ~ 4 whole eggs, separated
> ~ 2 or 3 extra egg whites

Prepare a 2-quart soufflé mold, coating it with cheese (page 203). Refrigerate.

Cook the rice in the milk, over a low heat, until tender, stirring frequently with a fork. When cooked properly, all the milk will have been absorbed. Set aside.

Stir the cheese into the lukewarm Béchamel, and stir in the cooked rice. With a wooden spatula, beat in the 4 egg yolks thoroughly, one at a time. Taste for seasoning. Beat the whites until they stand in firm peaks when you hold up the beater (page 201). Fold into the rice mixture gently. Pour into the prepared soufflé dish and bake in a preheated 375° F. oven for 40 to 45 minutes. Serve immediately. Serves 4 to 6.

An extraordinarily good luncheon soufflé, with a salad, followed by dessert.

* Make a thin Sauce Béchamel (see Glossary) in these proportions: 6 tablespoons butter, 3 tablespoons flour, 2 cups milk, and 1½ teaspoons salt.

CHICKEN SOUFFLÉ

This is an excellent way to use up the bits and pieces of cooked chicken that are not large enough to use for any other purpose.

> 4 tablespoons freshly grated Parmesan cheese
> 2 cups Sauce Velouté*
> ᗐ 4 whole eggs, separated
> ᗐ 2 or 3 extra egg whites
> 1½ to 2 cups finely diced chicken meat
> ½ cup heavy cream

Prepare a 1-quart soufflé mold, coating it with grated Parmesan cheese. Refrigerate.

Mix 2 tablespoons of the grated cheese into 1 cup of the hot sauce velouté. Cool. With a wire whisk, beat the 4 egg yolks one at a time into the sauce. (*The soufflé can be prepared to this point and set aside, sealed with Saran wrap.*)

Whip the egg whites until stiff but not dry (page 201), then whip about a third into the sauce vigorously. Mix in the chicken, then fold (page 202) in remainder of the beaten whites.

Spoon into the prepared soufflé mold, smooth the surface, and sprinkle with the remaining cheese. Bake in a preheated 375° F. oven for 25 to 30 minutes. Combine the remaining cup of sauce velouté with the cream, reheat but do not allow to boil, and serve with the soufflé. Serves 4.

* Make the Sauce Velouté (see Glossary) in these proportions: 6 tablespoons butter, 6 tablespoons flour, 2 cups rich chicken broth, seasoned with salt, freshly ground pepper, and freshly grated nutmeg.

CHICKEN-LIVER SOUFFLÉ

> 4 tablespoons butter
> 6 chicken livers
> 2 garlic cloves, minced
> 1 cup Sauce Béchamel*
> 5 parsley sprigs, chopped
> 4 whole eggs, separated
> 2 or 3 extra egg whites
> Olive and Mushroom Sauce (next page)

Prepare a 1-quart soufflé dish, coating it with fine bread crumbs (page 203). Refrigerate.

Melt half of the butter in a skillet and sauté the livers with the garlic, taking care not to burn the garlic, for about 5 minutes. Do not brown the livers. Chop the livers very fine and combine with the hot sauce Béchamel and the parsley. Cool slightly. With a wire whisk, beat the 4 egg yolks one by one into the Béchamel. (*The soufflé can be prepared to this point and set aside, sealed with Saran wrap.*)

Beat the egg whites until stiff but not dry (page 201). Whip about one third into the sauce vigorously. Fold (page 202) in the remainder. Pour into the prepared mold and bake in a preheated 375° F. oven for 30 to 35 minutes. Meanwhile make the sauce.

Serve the soufflé as soon as it is well puffed and browned and serve the sauce separately in a warm sauceboat. Serves 6.

* Make the Sauce Béchamel (see Glossary) in these proportions: 3 tablespoons butter, 3 tablespoons flour, 1 cup milk, seasoned with salt and freshly ground white pepper.

Olive and Mushroom Sauce

2 tablespoons butter
1 carrot, chopped
1 medium onion, chopped
1 garlic clove, chopped
3 tablespoons flour
2 cups chicken broth
1 cup (one 8-ounce can) tomato sauce
¼ teaspoon dried thyme
1 bay leaf
Salt
Freshly ground white pepper
½ cup pitted green olives
½ cup lightly sautéed mushrooms caps, sliced

Melt the butter and add the chopped carrot, onion and garlic. Cook over low heat until almost tender but not browned. Stir in the flour smoothly, then add the chicken broth, tomato sauce, thyme, bay leaf, and salt and pepper to taste. Cover tightly and cook over low heat for 30 minutes. Strain through a fine sieve into a clean saucepan. Add the olives and mushrooms. Put back over heat just long enough to heat through. The sauce, like the soufflé base, can be prepared ahead. Makes about 3 cups.

CHOCOLATE SOUFFLÉ

> 3 squares (1-ounce size) semisweet chocolate
> or ½ package (6-ounce size) chocolate pieces
> 2 tablespoons powdered instant coffee
> Crème Pâtissière (page 187) for which you
> need 4 egg yolks
> 7 egg whites
> Salt
> 1 tablespoon granulated sugar
> Sifted confectioners' sugar

Prepare a 1½-quart soufflé mold, coating it with granulated sugar (page 203). Refrigerate.

Melt the chocolate over hot, not boiling, water. Beat the melted chocolate and instant coffee thoroughly into the hot crème pâtissière. (*The soufflé can be prepared to this point and set aside, sealed with Saran wrap.*)

Beat the egg whites with a dash of salt until stiff but not dry (page 201), then beat in 1 tablespoon of granulated sugar. Whip about one third into the soufflé base very hard with a wire whip. Fold (page 202) in the remainder.

Bake in a preheated 375° F. oven for 35 minutes. Sprinkle confectioners' sugar through a fine sieve onto the surface of the soufflé and continue baking for 10 more minutes. Serve at once with Crème Chantilly (see Glossary). Serves 6.

Warning from Jacques: Chocolate soufflés are among the more difficult ones to make. "The chocolate is hard to go up," he says, suggesting that if you don't feel confident you may stir 1 tablespoon of arrowroot into the chocolate mixture just before you begin incorporating the beaten whites.

COFFEE SOUFFLÉ

∽ 4 whole eggs, separated
1 cup Sauce Béchamel*
2 tablespoons powdered instant coffee
∽ 2 or 3 extra egg whites
½ cup sugar
Coffee ice cream

Prepare a 1-quart soufflé mold (page 203), coating it with sugar. Refrigerate.

Beat the powdered instant coffee into the hot Béchamel. Cool slightly. With a whisk, beat in the 4 egg yolks one at a time. (*The soufflé can be prepared to this point and set aside, with a seal of Saran wrap.*)

Beat the egg whites until stiff but not dry (page 201), then beat in the sugar gradually, beating until you have a shiny smooth meringue. Whip about one third of the meringue into the coffee sauce vigorously with a wire whip. Fold (page 202) in the remaining whites.

Spoon into the prepared mold. Bake in a preheated 350° F. oven for 25 to 30 minutes. Serve with softened coffee ice cream as a sauce. Serves 4.

* Make the Sauce Béchamel (see Glossary) in these proportions: 1½ tablespoons butter, 4 tablespoons flour, 1 cup milk, a dash of salt.

LEMON SOUFFLÉ

> Grated rinds of 1½ lemons
> ¾ cup sugar
> ⅜ pound (1½ sticks) butter
> 9 whole eggs, separated
> Juice of 1½ lemons
> 2 extra egg whites
> Pinch of salt

Prepare a 1½-quart soufflé mold, coating it with sugar (page 203). Refrigerate. Grate the lemon rinds and set aside.

Combine the sugar, the butter cut into pieces, the egg yolks and lemon juice in the top of a double boiler. Place over simmering water and cook, stirring constantly with a wooden spatula, until mixture thickens noticeably. This takes quite a few minutes. Take off the heat, and beat until lukewarm. Stir in the lemon rind. (*The soufflé can be prepared to this point and set aside, with a seal of Saran wrap.*)

Beat the whites with the salt in a very large bowl until stiff but not dry (page 201). An electric mixer is very convenient when you have a mass of whites such as this to whip up.

Whip about one third of the beaten whites into the lemon base vigorously and thoroughly with a wire whip. Fold (page 202) in the remainder.

Pour into the prepared mold and bake in a preheated 325° F. oven for 30 to 35 minutes. Serves 6.

SOUFFLÉ À L'ORANGE

Crème Pâtissière (page 187), for which you
∾   need 4 egg yolks
Grated rind of 1 orange
2 tablespoons orange Curaçao
∾ 6 or 7 egg whites

Prepare a 1-quart soufflé mold, coating it with sugar (page 203).
Refrigerate.

Stir the orange rind and Curaçao into the crème pâtissière.
(*The soufflé can be prepared to this point and set aside, sealed
with Saran wrap.*) Beat the egg whites until stiff (page 201). Whip
about one third into the orange mixture with a wire whisk. Then
fold (page 202) in the remainder with a rubber spatula.

Pour into the prepared mold and bake in a preheated 375° F.
oven for 30 to 35 minutes, or until puffed and golden. Serves 3 to 4.

SOUFFLÉ ROTHSCHILD

⅔ cup mixed candied fruits
¼ cup kirsch
6 egg whites
Crème Pâtissière (page 187), for which you
need 4 egg yolks
Confectioners' sugar

Prepare a 1½-quart soufflé mold, coating it with sugar (page 203). Refrigerate.

Combine the candied fruits with the kirsch and allow to macerate. Beat the egg whites until stiff but not dry (page 201). Whip about one third into the cooled crème pâtissière vigorously with a wire whip. Fold in the fruits and kirsch with a spatula, then fold (page 202) in the remaining whites.

Pour into the prepared mold and bake in a preheated 375° F. oven for 20 minutes. Sprinkle with confectioners' sugar, shaking it through a small sieve over the top. Bake for another 10 to 15 minutes, or until soufflé has puffed to splendid heights and the top is nicely browned. Serve at once. Serves 6 to 8.

SOUFFLÉ GRAND MARNIER

> ~ 2 whole eggs, separated
> ½ recipe Crème Pâtissière (page 187), for
> ~ which you need 2 egg yolks
> ½ cup Grand Marnier
> ~ 3 extra egg whites

Prepare a 1-quart soufflé mold, coating it with granulated sugar (page 203). Refrigerate.

With a wire whisk, beat the 2 egg yolks one at a time into the cooled crème pâtissière. (*The soufflé can be prepared to this point and set aside, sealed with Saran wrap.*) Stir in the Grand Marnier. Beat the 5 egg whites until stiff but not dry (page 201). Whip about one third into the soufflé base vigorously. Fold (page 202) in the remainder.

Pour into the prepared mold and bake in a preheated 400° F. oven for 25 to 30 minutes. Serve immediately. Serves 6.

SOUFFLÉ AUX AMANDES

> ~ 6 whole eggs, separated
> 1 cup Sauce Béchamel*
> ~ 2 or 3 extra egg whites
> ½ cup sugar
> ½ teaspoon almond extract
> 3 tablespoons ground blanched almonds
> Sauce au Grand Marnier (below), for which
> ~ you need 2 egg yolks

* Make the Sauce Béchamel (see Glossary) in these proportions: 4 tablespoons butter, ½ cup flour and 1 cup milk.

Prepare a 1-quart soufflé mold (page 203), coating it with a mixture of half sugar and half flour. Refrigerate.

With a wire whisk, beat the 6 egg yolks one at a time into the lukewarm Béchamel. (*The soufflé can be prepared to this point and set aside, sealed with Saran wrap.*)

Beat the egg whites until stiff but not dry (page 201), then beat in the sugar gradually until you have a smooth shiny meringue. Stir in the almond extract. Whip about one third of the meringue into the yolk mixture vigorously with a wire whip. Fold (page 202) in the remaining whites.

Pour batter into the prepared mold and sprinkle the top with the ground almonds. Bake in a preheated 350° F. oven for 40 to 45 minutes.

When the soufflé is ready, serve it immediately with the chilled sauce below. Serves 6.

Sauce au Grand Marnier

1 cup heavy cream
2 egg yolks
2 tablespoons sugar
¼ teaspoon vanilla extract
1 jigger (3 tablespoons) Grand Marnier

Bring the cream to a boil. Beat together the egg yolks, sugar, and vanilla until the mixture makes "ribbons" (page 39). Whip the yolks gradually into the hot cream. Place the sauce over simmering water and stir with a wooden spatula until it coats the spatula. Chill in the refrigerator. Add the Grand Marnier just before serving. Makes about 1½ cups.

Index